# Microsoft Application Virtualization Cookbook

Over 55 hands-on recipes covering the key aspects of a successful App-V deployment

**James Preston**

BIRMINGHAM - MUMBAI

# Microsoft Application Virtualization Cookbook

First published: August 2015

Production reference: 1100815

Published by Packt Publishing Ltd.
Livery Place
35 Livery Street
Birmingham B3 2PB, UK.

ISBN 978-1-78528-104-4

www.packtpub.com

# Credits

**Author**

James Preston

**Reviewers**

Husain Chomelawala

Mayur Arvind Makwana

Matthew M. Spencer

**Commissioning Editor**

Ashwin Nair

**Acquisition Editor**

Usha Iyer

**Content Development Editor**

Gaurav Sharma

**Technical Editor**

Abhishek R. Kotian

**Copy Editors**

Pranjali Chury

Brandt D'Mello

**Project Coordinator**

Harshal Ved

**Proofreader**

Safis Editing

**Indexer**

Monica Ajmera Mehta

**Production Coordinator**

Arvindkumar Gupta

**Cover Work**

Arvindkumar Gupta

# About the Author

**James Preston** is an IT professional working in the field of education and has a broad range of interests, including virtualization with Hyper-V and App-V, data-orientated application design with Visual Studio Lightswitch, IP telephony, and remote access technologies.

Willing to share this breadth of knowledge, he runs a personal blog (`myworldofit.net`), which covers a wide range of topics; this most recently includes an end-to-end deployment of Microsoft Hyper-V Server 2012 R2, publishing a WebDAV server, the effective integration of student databases with virtual learning environments, and a take on an enterprise Wi-Fi deployment.

James has previously provided technical reviews for books on Microsoft Hyper-V and Citrix® VDI-In-A-Box.

When not working, he can be found in a local coffee shop, having a go at the latest computer games or planning the training program for his local Air Cadet squadron.

# About the Reviewers

**Husain Chomelawala** is an expert in the field of application packaging, virtualization, and deployment technologies with 6 years of experience. His experience includes working on App-V, Admin Studio, Installshield, Vmware Vsphere, Hyper-V, and Citrix® solutions. He is presently leading an application packaging and virtualization project in one of the Fortune 500 companies.

I would like to thank three very special ladies in my life: my mom, Fatema; my wife, Arwa; and my sweet little daughter, Fatema, for their support and inspiration. Special thanks to my father and mentor, Asgarali Chomelawala, for all his continuing guidance and support. Thanks Packt Publishing for giving me this opportunity.

**Mayur Arvind Makwana** is a software professional who holds a degree in computer engineering and has more than 6 years of experience in the field of information technology, covering Microsoft, Citrix®, and VMware technologies. Presently, he is leading a project on Citrix® (XenApp/Xendesktop) and Windows (WSUS/SCCM) in one of leading Fortune 500 companies. He is a huge believer in certifications with his current certifications, including the following:

- Citrix Certified Administrator for Citrix® XenApp 6.5 (CCA)
- Microsoft Certified Professional (MCP)
- Microsoft Specialist (Microsoft Server Virtualization with Windows Server Hyper-V and System Center)
- VMware Certified Associate - Data Center Virtualization (VCA-DCV)
- Information Technology Infrastructure Library (ITIL) V3 Foundation
- ChangeBase AOK (Application Compatibility Testing and Remediation)
- Oracle Certified Associate (OCA)

He also reviews technical books and writes technical blogs. He has attended several courses and conducted a lot of training, some of them are as follows:

- Licensing Windows Server
- Advanced Tools & Scripting with PowerShell 3.0 Jump Start
- Deploying Windows 8
- Licensing Windows 8
- Migrating from Windows XP to Windows 7
- Networking Fundamentals
- An introduction to Hyper-V Jump Start
- Adminstudio 2014
- APPV/VMware ThinAPP/Citrix® Profiling

He has also worked on *Getting Started With PowerShell,* by Packt Publishing. You can visit his blog as well, www.all-about-software-applications-repackaging.com.

I would like to thank my mom, Beena Makwana, who has always encouraged me to utilize my potential and help people by sharing my expertise and knowledge. Thanks to the team at Packt Publishing for giving me this opportunity.

**Matthew M. Spencer** is currently an architect, analyst, writer, and consultant. His career spans over 15 years across universities, state government organizations, software leaders, healthcare institutions, small businesses, and the Fortune 500 companies. His work specializes in creating solutions to complex problems.

Matthew's projects have received many awards and accolades. Some of his proudest career achievements include an implementation of a multilingual collaboration and content management solution to 18,000 global users. He also created a SaaS (Software as a Service) application for the state government to sell technical services to other state and local governments that interface with the FBI. Most recently, he advanced to the second round of Verizon's Powerful Answers Award competition and was recently nominated to speak at TEDx.

He often tweets about technology at `@chivalry` and can also be found at `mattspencer.net`. He enjoys travelling the world, running endurance races, brewing his own beer, and contributing to The Good Judgment Project. He lives with his family in West Virginia.

I would like to thank my loving wife, Lisa Go, and my daughter, Isabella, for their support and patience throughout this project. I would also like to pay special gratitude to my mentor, teacher, and dear friend, Bob Pirner, for his continuous guidance and support.

# www.PacktPub.com

## Support files, eBooks, discount offers, and more

For support files and downloads related to your book, please visit www.PacktPub.com.

Did you know that Packt offers eBook versions of every book published, with PDF and ePub files available? You can upgrade to the eBook version at www.PacktPub.com and as a print book customer, you are entitled to a discount on the eBook copy. Get in touch with us at service@packtpub.com for more details.

At www.PacktPub.com, you can also read a collection of free technical articles, sign up for a range of free newsletters and receive exclusive discounts and offers on Packt books and eBooks.

https://www2.packtpub.com/books/subscription/packtlib

Do you need instant solutions to your IT questions? PacktLib is Packt's online digital book library. Here, you can search, access, and read Packt's entire library of books.

## Why subscribe?

- ▶ Fully searchable across every book published by Packt
- ▶ Copy and paste, print, and bookmark content
- ▶ On demand and accessible via a web browser

## Free access for Packt account holders

If you have an account with Packt at www.PacktPub.com, you can use this to access PacktLib today and view 9 entirely free books. Simply use your login credentials for immediate access.

## Instant updates on new Packt books

Get notified! Find out when new books are published by following @PacktEnterprise on Twitter or the *Packt Enterprise* Facebook page.

# Table of Contents

# Preface

Microsoft first entered the Application Virtualization world in 2006 with the purchase of Softricity. At its core, App-V allows administrators to easily deploy applications in the form of packages to users without having to use traditional deployment methods.

App-V 5 (originally launched in 2012) is a generational step up from the previous versions with the introduction of the .appv extension for packages and the removal of the need to specify a package root at the time of sequencing. Since then, Microsoft has continued to enhance App-V through service packs, the most recent of which has greatly improved the connections group feature, which allows virtual applications to share components with each other.

In this book, you will discover a range of ways to utilize App-V to meet the particular needs of your deployment through step-by-step instructions.

## What this book covers

*Chapter 1*, *Deploying App-V 5 Services*, covers the steps to get your backend App-V infrastructure up and running. Here, we cover everything from the installation of a SQL server and the creation of a redundant Publishing server to two options on how to store your APPV files.

*Chapter 2*, *Deploying App-V 5 Clients and Updates*, leverages your existing skills (or teaches you new ones!) in Group Policy software deployment and Microsoft System Centre Configuration Manager to deploy the App-V client prerequisites, client, and updates to your end users.

*Chapter 3*, *Sequencing Applications*, illustrates the steps to set up your sequencing PC and use a range of methods to capture applications in App-V packages.

*Chapter 4*, *Managing Packages*, covers deploying packages to your end users while managing file type associations and shortcut paths.

*Chapter 5*, *Using Connection Groups*, captures a middleware package (the Java Development Kit) and joins it with another virtual application to share application components.

*Chapter 6, Sequencing Office 2013*, utilizes the new scripted approach to obtaining a package for Office 2013 and reduces the time taken for deployment.

*Chapter 7, Deploying App-V 5 in a Virtual Environment*, covers how to take advantage of the Shared Content Store mode to further enhance your Remote Desktop Services or Citrix® XenDesktop® environment with App-V.

*Chapter 8, Managing Packages in System Center Configuration Manager 2012 R2*, covers extending your SCCM infrastructure to deploy App-V packages to your users without the need for any further App-V infrastructure.

*Chapter 9, Reporting in App-V 5*, covers helpful insights on the state of your App-V clients and lets you know which applications are being run using the App-V Reporting Server and Microsoft Office Excel.

*Chapter 10, Troubleshooting*, lets you know where to go when it all goes wrong. This demonstrates identifying the correct App-V logging and getting your users back up and running in no time.

# What you need for this book

At its core, this book uses a number of machines running Microsoft Windows Server 2012 R2, App-V 5 SP3, and management PCs running Windows 8.1. To take full advantage of later chapters as the book progresses, you also require access to System Centre Configuration Manager 2012 R2 and Citrix® XenDesktop® 7.6.

For the purposes of a test environment, the full infrastructure as described in this cookbook can be provisioned on any modern desktop PC with a VirtualBox (or Hyper-V client) instance, a quad-core processor, 32 GB of RAM, and a 500 GB hard drive.

# Who this book is for

If you have some experience with App-V but are overwhelmed by the range of features on offer, then this book is for you. A basic understanding of App-V and common Windows server technologies (Active Directory/Group Policy/PowerShell) is necessary.

# Sections

In this book, you will find several headings that appear frequently (Getting ready, How to do it, How it works, There's more, and See also).

To give clear instructions on how to complete a recipe, we use these sections as follows:

## Getting ready

This section tells you what to expect in the recipe, and describes how to set up any software or any preliminary settings required for the recipe.

## How to do it...

This section contains the steps required to follow the recipe.

## How it works...

This section usually consists of a detailed explanation of what happened in the previous section.

## There's more...

This section consists of additional information about the recipe in order to make the reader more knowledgeable about the recipe.

## See also

This section provides helpful links to other useful information for the recipe.

# Conventions

In this book, you will find a number of styles of text that distinguish between different kinds of information. Here are some examples of these styles, and an explanation of their meaning.

Code words in text, database table names, folder names, filenames, file extensions, pathnames, dummy URLs, user input, and Twitter handles are shown as follows: "We can include other contexts through the use of the `include` directive."

A block of code is set as follows:

```
Windows Registry Editor Version 5.00

[HKEY_LOCAL_MACHINE\SYSTEM\CurrentControlSet\Services\InetInfo\
Parameters]
"ObjectCacheTTL"=dword:000004b0
"MaxCachedFileSizeInMB"=dword:00001000
```

Any command-line input or output is written as follows:

```
setup.exe /packager .\configuration.xml "\\demo.org\app-v\Office 2013
```

**New terms** and **important words** are shown in bold. Words that you see on the screen, in menus or dialog boxes for example, appear in the text like this: "Under the **Domain Groups** OU create the following Security Groups."

 Warnings or important notes appear in a box like this.

Tips and tricks appear like this.

# Reader feedback

Feedback from our readers is always welcome. Let us know what you think about this book—what you liked or may have disliked. Reader feedback is important for us to develop titles that you really get the most out of.

To send us general feedback, simply send an e-mail to feedback@packtpub.com, and mention the book title via the subject of your message.

If there is a topic that you have expertise in and you are interested in either writing or contributing to a book, see our author guide on www.packtpub.com/authors.

# Customer support

Now that you are the proud owner of a Packt book, we have a number of things to help you to get the most from your purchase.

## Downloading the example code

You can download the example code files for all Packt books you have purchased from your account at http://www.packtpub.com. If you purchased this book elsewhere, you can visit http://www.packtpub.com/support and register to have the files e-mailed directly to you.

## Errata

Although we have taken every care to ensure the accuracy of our content, mistakes do happen. If you find a mistake in one of our books—maybe a mistake in the text or the code—we would be grateful if you would report this to us. By doing so, you can save other readers from frustration and help us improve subsequent versions of this book. If you find any errata, please report them by visiting http://www.packtpub.com/submit-errata, selecting your book, clicking on the **errata submission form** link, and entering the details of your errata. Once your errata are verified, your submission will be accepted and the errata will be uploaded on our website, or added to any list of existing errata, under the Errata section of that title. Any existing errata can be viewed by selecting your title from http://www.packtpub.com/support.

## Piracy

Piracy of copyright material on the Internet is an ongoing problem across all media. At Packt, we take the protection of our copyright and licenses very seriously. If you come across any illegal copies of our works, in any form, on the Internet, please provide us with the location address or website name immediately so that we can pursue a remedy.

Please contact us at copyright@packtpub.com with a link to the suspected pirated material.

We appreciate your help in protecting our authors, and our ability to bring you valuable content.

## Questions

You can contact us at questions@packtpub.com if you are having a problem with any aspect of the book, and we will do our best to address it.

# 1
# Deploying App-V 5 Services

In this chapter, we will cover:

- ▸  Obtaining the App-V installers
- ▸  Configuring Active directory
- ▸  Configuring a distributed filesystem
- ▸  Configuring Internet Information Services
- ▸  Configuring SQL Server
- ▸  Deploying a standalone management and publishing server
- ▸  Accessing the management console
- ▸  Adding additional administrators
- ▸  Deploying a second Publishing server

## Introduction

Microsoft Application Virtualization 5 (**App-V 5**) enables system administrators to deliver applications to end users in a consistent and efficient manner without the hassle of traditional deployment methods.

The individual components of App-V 5 can be used in a variety of combinations to meet your particular needs. A full App-V 5 server deployment would employ the following services:

| App-V 5 component | Description |
|---|---|
| The management server and database | This provides a web-based console used by authorized administrators to publish applications. All this information is stored in a SQL Server. |
| The publishing server | This authenticates the clients, and in return, provides the list of authorized applications and the SMB/HTTP paths to the servers. |
| The file server/web server | Applications are stored on a file or web server, or even on a combination of the two. |
| The client | This presents applications to users and caches those applications on the client for later use. |

The flexible nature of App-V also allows for applications to be deployed through **Microsoft System Centre Configuration Manager** (**SCCM**) as well as through **Electronic Software Distribution,** for example, with Group Policy assignments. In this cookbook, we will cover these alternative deployment methods in later chapters.

We will use the following IP addresses and hostnames in order to cover the full range of deployment options. Each server runs **Windows Server 2012 R2** on the 255.255.248.0 subnet. These servers can be configured as virtual or physical machines. I suggest that you use vCPU, RAM, and storage allocations for the demo environment, which can also be found in the following table:

| IP Address | Hostname | vCPU | RAM | Storage |
|---|---|---|---|---|
| **172.16.0.1** | (default gateway) | N/A | N/A | N/A |
| **172.16.0.2** | DC | 2 | 2GB | 40GB |
| **172.16.0.3** | FS1 | 2 | 2GB | 80GB |
| **172.16.0.4** | FS2 | 2 | 2GB | 80GB |
| **172.16.0.5** | WEB1 | 2 | 2GB | 80GB |
| **172.16.0.6** | WEB2 | 2 | 2GB | 80GB |
| **172.16.0.7** | RDS | 4 | 4GB | 80GB |
| **172.16.0.8** | APPV1 | 2 | 2GB | 40GB |
| **172.16.0.9** | APPV2 | 2 | 2GB | 40GB |
| **172.16.0.10** | SCCM | 4 | 8GB | 100GB |

The 172.16.0.12 and 172.16.0.13 IP Addresses should be reserved for use with **Network Load Balancing** (**NLB**).

In addition, you will need to create a number of Windows 8.1 clients for the sequencing and testing of applications as well as to access the App-V management console.

 Note that the specifications in the preceding table are only suitable for a demo environment. For your production environment, consult the App-V 5.0 Capacity Planning page at `https://technet.microsoft.com/en-gb/library/dn595131.aspx`.

# Obtaining the App-V installers

This recipe provides the links to download the App-V 5 installers.

## Getting ready

It is assumed that you have a valid Microsoft account and have purchased the **Microsoft Desktop Optimization Pack** (**MDOP**) as part of **Volume License Agreement**. Depending on your subscription level, you may also have access to the App-V installers as part of a **Microsoft Developer Network** (**MSDN**) subscription.

## How to do it...

The following list shows you the fundamental steps involved in this recipe and the tasks required to complete the recipe:

1.  Download MDOP.

2.  Browse to the **Microsoft Volume Licensing Service Centre** website (`https://www.microsoft.com/licensing/servicecenter`).

3.  Navigate to the **Downloads and Keys** option.

4.  In the product filter, search for **Microsoft Desktop Optimization Pack for Software Assurance 2014 R2**.

5. Select **Download** and then click on **Continue** to begin the download. Ensure that you save the ISO file to a memorable location:

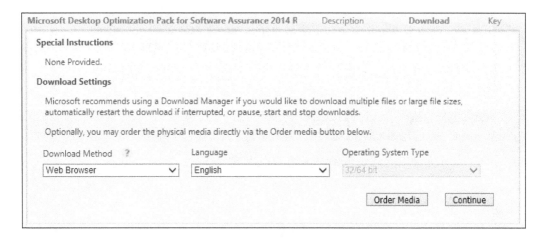

 Note that a product key is not required for App-V 5.

Microsoft App-V 5 Service Pack 3 supports Microsoft SQL Server 2008, 2008 R2, and 2012 for use with the management server database and the reporting server database. A full list of supported configurations can be found at `http://technet.microsoft.com/en-gb/library/jj713426.aspx`.

# Configuring Active Directory

This recipe shows you the **Active Directory** configuration on a domain controller that will be used through this cookbook. In addition, it shows the configuration of a **Group Policy Object** (**GPO**) that will allow traffic through the firewall of Windows servers.

## Getting ready

It is assumed that you have access rights to create objects in Active Directory, including **Organizational Units** (**OUs**), security groups, and user accounts.

## How to do it...

The following list shows you the fundamental tasks involved in this recipe and the tasks required to complete the recipe (all of the actions in this recipe will take place on the server with the hostname DC):

- ▸ Creating required OUs
- ▸ Creating required security groups
- ▸ Creating required computer accounts and user accounts
- ▸ Creating a new GPO and linking it to an OU
- ▸ Configuring the GPO with a Windows firewall policy

The implementation of the preceding steps is as follows:

1. Create the following OUs and pre-provision the computer accounts as shown:

2. Under the **Domain Groups** OU, create the following Security Groups:

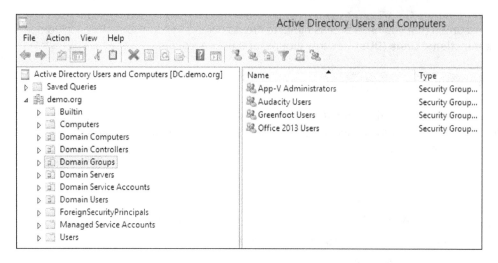

3. Under **Domain Users**, create the following user accounts. In addition to this, add **Sam Adams** to the **App-V Administrators Security Group** option:

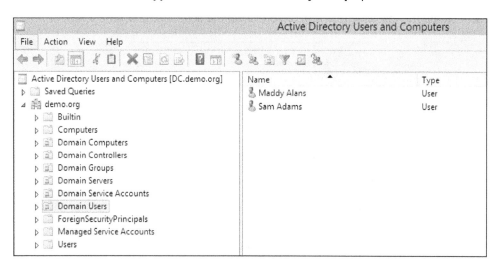

4. Open the **Group Policy Management Console (GPMC)** console, expand the OU tree to show **Domain Servers**, and then right-click on the **App-V Servers** OU. From the menu that appears, click on **Create a GPO in this domain, and Link it here**.

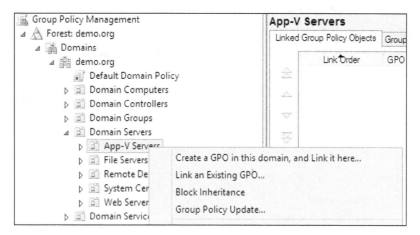

5. In the dialogue box that appears, enter `Allow 440-442` as the name and click on **OK**.

6. In the new window that appears, right-click on the **policies title** option, and from the menu that appears, click on **Properties**.

7. Tick the **Disable User Configuration settings** checkbox and click on **OK**:

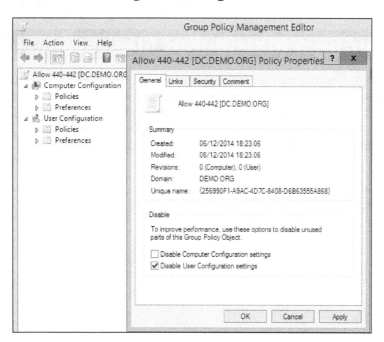

8. Expand the tree structure to navigate to **Computer Configuration | Policies | Windows Settings | Security Settings | Windows Firewall with Advanced Security | Windows Firewall with Advanced Security – LDAP**.

9. Right-click on **Inbound Rules** and select **New Rule**.

10. In the window that appears, select the **Port radio** option and click on **Next**.

11. Leave **TCP** selected, enter `440-442` in the **Specific local ports** box, and click on **Next**.

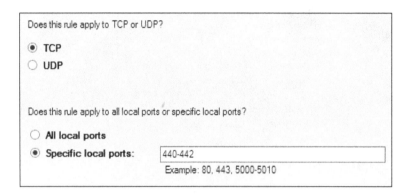

12. Leave **Allow the connection** selected and click on **Next**.

13. Remove the ticks from **Private** and **Public** to leave only **Domain** checked. Now, click on **Next**.

14. Finally, give the policy the name `Allow 440-442`, and click on **Finish**.

# Configuring a distributed filesystem

Microsoft App-V 5 packages can be stored on a Windows share or on a web server. Using a **Distributed File System** (**DFS**) namespace to host App-V packages allows you to scale out your infrastructure or move the packages between servers at a later date, if required, without the burden of updating the paths to the App-V database. Using **Distributed File System Replication** (**DFS-R**) allows you to host the packages (and keep those packages in sync) on multiple servers for redundancy.

In this recipe, we will create two DFS namespaces: `FileStore` for general purpose use and `App-V` for hosting the App-V packages.

## Getting ready

This recipe assumes that you have provisioned and domain-joined two file servers with the names `FS1` and `FS2`, respectively. It is suggested that a unique namespace be used to host the packages.

## How to do it...

The following list shows you the fundamental tasks involved in this recipe and the tasks required to complete the recipe:

- ▶ Install the DFS and DFS-R roles on FS1 and FS2
- ▶ Create the `FileStore` namespace on FS1
- ▶ Enable replication between FS1 and FS2
- ▶ Join FS2 to the FileStore namespace
- ▶ Create the App-V namespace and replication group on FS1 and FS2

The implementation of the preceding steps is as follows:

1.  Start by installing the DFS and DFS-R features on FS1 and FS2. This can be performed from a **PowerShell** prompt by entering the following command:

    ```
    Install-WindowsFeature -Name FS-DFS-Namespace, FS-DFS-Replication
    -IncludeManagementTools -Restart
    ```

2.  Once the installation is complete (and the server is restarted if required), navigate to the start screen from the applications list, and under **Administrative Tools**, click on **DFS Management** to launch the DFS management console.

3.  In the new window that appears, click on **New Namespace...** to create a new DFS namespace.

4.  In the **New Namespace Wizard** window, enter **FS1** as the server that will host the namespace, and click on **Next**.

5.  Enter **FileStore** as the name of the namespace, click on **Edit Settings**. In the window that appears, set `C:\DFSRoots\FileStore` as the local path to the shared folder and set the shared folder permissions to **custom** with the **Everyone** security group having read only access and the App-V Administrators having full access. Click on **Next**.

6. Leave the domain-based namespace selected with the **Enable Windows Server 2008** mode tick box checked. Now click on **Next**:

> Select the type of namespace to create.
>
> ⦿ Domain-based namespace
>
> A domain-based namespace is stored on one or more namespace servers and in Active Directory Domain Services. You can increase the availability of a domain-based namespace by using multiple servers. When created in Windows Server 2008 mode, the namespace supports increased scalability and access-based enumeration.
>
> ☑ Enable Windows Server 2008 mode
>
> Preview of domain-based namespace:
>
> \\demo.org\FileStore

Using **Windows Server 2008** mode with your DFS namespace allows your namespace to utilize access-based enumeration, as well as support for clusters.

7. Review the settings and then click on **Create** to set up the namespace.

8. When the final page confirms that the setup is completed successfully, click on **Close**.

9. With the DFS namespace created, we will now create a replication group between FS1 and FS2. This will automatically replicate changes between the two file servers.

10. In the DFS management console, click on **New Replication Group...**.

11. In the window that appears, leave the **Multipurpose replication group selected** option selected and click on **Next**.

12. Set the name of the replication group as **FileStore** and click on **Next**.

13. On the **Replication Group Members** screen, add both **FS1** and **FS2**, and click on **Next**.

14. Leave **Full mesh** selected on the topology screen and click on **Next**.

15. On the **Schedule and Bandwidth** screen, leave the default settings as they are and click on **Next**.

16. Set **FS1** in the **Primary member** option of the replication group and click on **Next**:

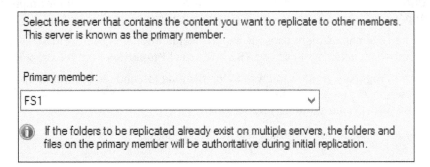

17. Add `C:\DFSRoots\FileStore` as the path for the replicated folder on **FS1** (the one created in step 5 in this recipe) and click on **Next**.

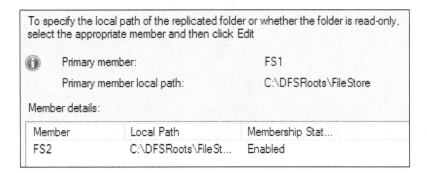

18. At the **Local Path** option of **FileStore** on the **Other Members** screen, set the path of **FS2** as **C:\DFSRoots\FileStore**, click on **Next**.

Allowing DFS to create the folder for you removes the need to create the folder manually.

19. Review the settings that will be used to create the replication group and click on **Create**.

20. You will then receive confirmation that the replication group has been created successfully. Click on **Close** to finish the wizard.

21. Before joining FS2 to the DFS namespace, you must increase the size of the **Staging Quota** option on the replication group. This allows for large files (for example, whole App-V packages or ISOs) to replicate between the servers successfully.

22. In the DFS management console, expand **Replication** and select **FileStore**. In the memberships tab, right-click on **FS1** and select **Properties** from the drop-down menu.

23. In the **Properties** window, browse to the **Staging** tab and set the **Quota** option to the size of the largest file that you will be storing on your file server (for example, 8192 MB). Do the same for **FS2** as well.

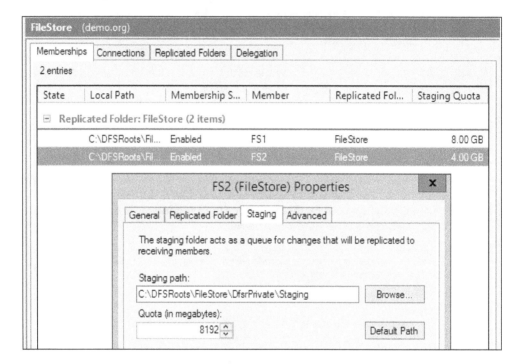

 By way of example, Office 2013 with Visio and a single language pack is approximately 1.2 GB in size, while the Adobe CS6 suite is up to 4 GB. Ensure that you continue to review the size of your staging quota as your use of App-V increases to ensure that the single largest file will always be able to replicate.

24. We will now add FS2 to the namespace. Doing this provides redundancy in the namespace, allowing for FS1 to fail without impacting your clients.

25. In the DFS management console, expand namespaces and select the **FileStore** namespace that you created earlier. Select the **Namespace Servers** tab and note that only **FS1** is listed. On the right-hand side of the window, click on **Add Namespace Server...**.

26. In the window that appears, set **FS2** as the **Namespace server** option and click on **Edit Settings**:

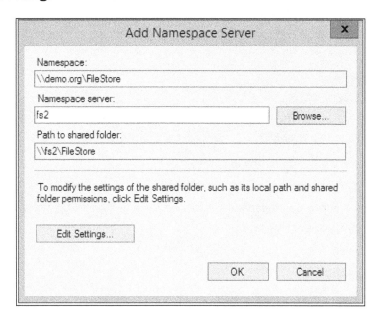

27. Set `C:\DFSRoots\FileStore` as the path and use custom permissions with the **Everyone** security group set as `read only`, and the **App-V Administrators** security group set to full control.

28. Click on **OK** to close the **Edit Settings** window, and then click on **OK** again to add FS2 to the namespace.

29. Finally, set the NTFS permissions on the **FileStore** to allow everyone to read the contents of the folder and for App-V Administrators to have full control over the folder.

30. To complete this recipe, repeat steps 3 to 26 using App-V as the name of the namespace with the file path set as `C:\DFSRoots\App-V` and replication enabled for that folder between FS1 and FS2.

# Configuring Internet information services

As an alternative to using a simple DFS share, you can also host App-V packages on an **Internet Information Services** (**IIS**) web server. Doing this gives you the added benefit of caching the App-V packages in RAM, which allows for multiple loads of the same package on multiple clients to be faster than just hosting the package on a network share.

Using NLB and hosting the packages on a DFS share allows the web servers to have a fault-tolerant configuration.

## Getting ready

This recipe assumes that you have provisioned and domain-joined two web servers with the names WEB1 and WEB2, respectively. You will need administrative permissions on both WEB1 and WEB2 as well as the ability to create a DNS entry.

## How to do it...

The following list shows you the fundamental steps involved in this recipe and the tasks required to complete this recipe:

- ▸ Provision a DNS entry for the load balancer
- ▸ Install the required Windows server roles on WEB1 and WEB2
- ▸ Create the App-VIIS namespace and replication group on WEB1 and WEB2
- ▸ Configure Network Load Balancing
- ▸ Configure IIS
- ▸ Configure caching

The implementation of the preceding steps is as follows:

1. On DC, launch the DNS management console, expand **Forward Lookup Zones**, and right-click on your domain. From the drop-down menu, select **New Host (A or AAAA)...**.

2. Set the name to `appv` and the **IP address** option to `172.16.0.12`. Click on **Add Host** to create the record:

3. On WEB1 and WEB2, launch PowerShell and run the following command to install the DFS and DFS-R roles along with NLB and IIS:

```
Install-WindowsFeature -Name FS-DFS-Namespace, FS-DFS-Replication,
Web-Default-Doc, Web-Dir-Browsing, Web-Http-Errors, Web-Static-
Content, Web-App-Dev, Web-Http-Logging, Web-Request-Monitor, Web-
Performance, NLB -IncludeManagementTools -Restart
```

4. After allowing the server to restart if required, launch the DFS management console on WEB1, and using steps 3 to 26 of the previous recipe, provision a DFS namespace and replication group with the name App-VIIS and the folder path set to `C:\DFSRoots\App-VIIS` on WEB1 and WEB2. This namespace and replication group will be used to host the App-V packages on the web servers; however, IIS will be used to present the files to the clients.

5. We will now configure NLB between WEB1 and WEB2; doing this provides redundancy between the two servers and ensures that under normal conditions, neither server is overloaded with requests.

6. From the **Start** screen, launch the **Network Load Balancing Manager** software:

7. In the window that appears, select **Cluster** and then click on **New**.

8. In the **New Cluster** option, connect window enter WEB1 as the host and click on **Connect**. From the list of interfaces, select the interface with the IP address 172.16.0.5 and click on **Next**.

 In this evaluation environment, only a single network interface has been configured. In a production environment, you would want to have two interfaces, one for the management of the server and another purely for NLB traffic.

9. From the **Host Parameters** screen, leave the default settings in place and click on **Next**.

10. On the **Cluster IP Address** screen, add a new IP address and set the **IPv4 address** option to 172.16.0.12 with 255.255.248.0 as the **Subnet mask** option:

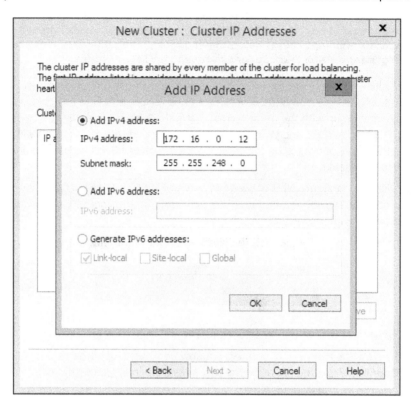

11. At the **Cluster Parameters** option, leave `172.16.0.12` as the IP address and set the **Full Internet** name to `appv.demo.org` (as set in step 1 of this recipe). Also, set the **Cluster operation** mode to **Multicast** and click on **Next**.

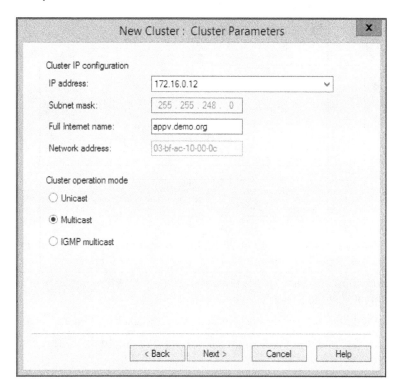

 If you are using hosts with a management and an NLB network adapter, select **Unicast** as the **Cluster operation** mode.

12. Accept the default configuration for **Port Rules** and click on **Finish** to create the cluster.

13. To add WEB2 to the cluster, expand **Network Load Balancing Clusters**, right-click on **appv.demo.org (172.16.0.12)**, and click on **Add Host To Cluster**:

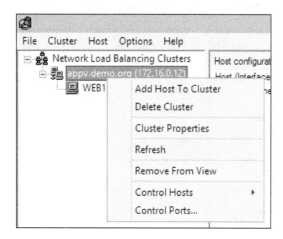

14. In the window that appears, set WEB2 as the host and click on **Connect**. In the interface with the IP address **172.16.0.6** selected, click on **Next**.

15. At the host parameters, accept the defaults (note that the unique host identifier of this server is set to 2) and click on **Next**.

16. Accept the defaults for the **Port Rules** option and click on **Finish**.

17. After a short wait, the two hosts will enter the **Converged** state. This completes the setup of the NLB cluster.

| Host configuration information for hosts in cluster appv.demo.org (172.16.0.12) | | | | | |
|---|---|---|---|---|---|
| Host (Interface) | Status | Dedicated IP address | Dedicated IP subnet mask | Host priority | Initial host state |
| WEB1(Ethernet) | Converged | 172.16.0.5 | 255.255.248.0 | 1 | started |
| WEB2(Ethernet) | Converged | 172.16.0.6 | 255.255.248.0 | 2 | started |

We will now configure the IIS web server on WEB1.

1. From the Start screen, launch the **Internet Information Services management** console:

2. Expand the **WEB1** option, go to the **Sites** option and then right-click on the **Default Web Site** option and click on **Remove**.

3. Click on **Application Pools**, right-click on **DefaultAppPool**, and click on **Remove**.

4. Right-click on **Sites** and click on **Add Website...**

5. In the **Add Website...** window, set the **Physical path** option to the DFS root that you created earlier (C:\DFSRoots\App-VIIS) and the **Host name** to **appv.demo.org**. Leave **Start Website immediately** checked and click on **OK**.

6. To allow the server to handle the .appv file type, select WEB1 from the connection tree and then double-click on **MIME Types** in the **Features View** option:

7. In the **MIME Types** window, click on **Add....** In the window that appears, set the **File name** extension as `.appv` and the **MIME Types** option as `application/appv`.

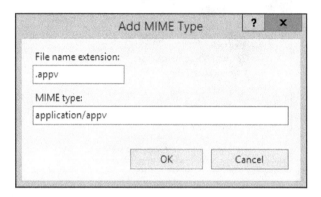

8. With IIS configured, we will now set the file cache on the server to allow for large files (up to 4096 MB) to be stored in RAM when served through the web server.

9. On WEB1, open Notepad from the Start screen and enter the following:

```
Windows Registry Editor Version 5.00

[HKEY_LOCAL_MACHINE\SYSTEM\CurrentControlSet\Services\
InetInfo\Parameters]
"ObjectCacheTTL"=dword:000004b0
"MaxCachedFileSizeInMB"=dword:00001000
```

10. Save the Notepad file to the desktop with the name `updatecache.reg`, and then double-click on it to run the file; this will in turn add the entries to the registry under the `HKEY_LOCAL_MACHINE\SYSTEM\CurrentControlSet\Services\InetInfo\Parameters` parameter.

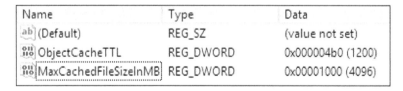

 These additional registry entries extend the file cache up to 4096 MB and allow objects to stay in the cache for up to 120 seconds. Although 4096 is the largest object that can be in the cache, you can extend the period for which it will stay in the cache by altering the `ObjectCacheTTL` value.

11. Finally, open the `C:\Windows\system32\inetsrv\config\applicationHost.config` file in Notepad, search for `<serverRuntime />`, and replace it with the following:

```
<serverRuntime frequentHitTimePeriod="00:00:01"
frequentHitThreshold="1" />
```

12. The `frequentHitThreshold` parameter determines how many hits the file receives before it is cached (in this case, only one hit is required), and the `frequentHitTimePeriod` value determines how many hits the file receives in a time period before it is cached (in this case, in a single second).

# Configuring SQL Server

Microsoft SQL Server is required to host the App-V Management and Reporting databases. With the exception of very large deployments of App-V, SQL server can be collocated on the App-V Management Server (and on the Publishing server as well).

## Getting ready

This recipe assumes that you have provisioned and domain-joined a server with the name APPV1, and that you have a valid licence to install Microsoft SQL Server 2008, 2008 R2, or 2012 at the Standard, Enterprise, Datacenter, or Developer Edition levels. Note that the Express edition is not supported.

## How to do it...

Here are the fundamental steps involved in this recipe:

1. Install and configure a default setup of SQL Server.

2. Launch the **SQL Setup** application, select **Installation** and **New SQL Server stand-alone installation or add features to an existing installation**.

3. Allow the **Setup Support Rules** check to complete and click on **OK**.

4. Enter your product key and click on **Next**.

5. Review the terms of the licensing agreement, tick the **I accept the license terms** box, and click on **Next**.

6. Allow the **Setup Support Rules** check to finish. At this stage, you might have a warning on Windows Firewall stating that certain ports are not open. This can be safely ignored as we are hosting the App-V Management server and SQL server on the same machine. Click on **Next**.

7. On the **Setup Role** screen, select **SQL Server Feature Installation** and click on **Next**.

8. On the **Feature Selection** screen, tick the **Database Engine Services** option and click on **Next**.

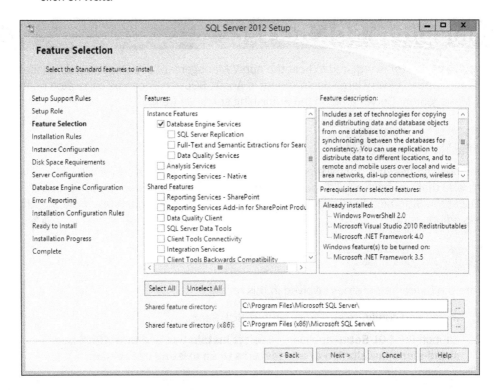

 Note that no other SQL Server features are required for App-V; however, you may install the Complete Management Tools set to allow you to examine the contents of the App-V Management database.

9. Allow the **Installation Rules** check to complete and click on **Next**.

10. Leave the **Default instance** option selected with **Instance ID** set to **MSSQLSERVER**. Click on **Next**.

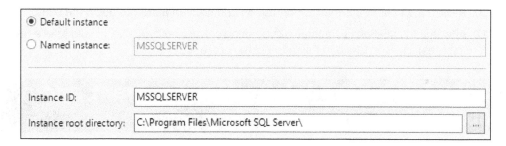

11. Review the **Disk Space Requirements** check and click on **Next**.

12. Accept the defaults for the **Service Accounts** option and click on **Next**.

13. On the **Database Engine Configuration** set, select **Windows authentication** mode and click on **Add Current User** to make the account that you are logged in with an administrator on SQL Server. You must use the same account to install the App-V Management Server in the next recipe.

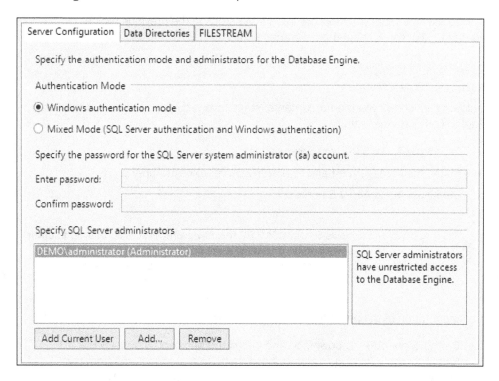

14. On the **Error Reporting** page, accept the defaults and click on **Next**.

15. Review the **Installation Configuration Rules** check and click on **Next**.

16. Review the final SQL Server configuration and click on **Install** to begin the setup.

17. After the installation is complete (depending on your hardware this could take a few minutes), click on **Close** to finish the setup process.

# Deploying a standalone Management and a Publishing server

In a typical App-V 5 deployment, you will deploy a Management server that stores information about packages, applications, file types, and shortcuts in SQL server (as set up in the previous recipe). In turn, Publishing servers regularly poll the management server for a compiled list of these applications and settings to present authenticated requests to the clients. In this recipe, you will deploy a standalone Management and Publishing server.

## Getting ready

This recipe assumes that you have completed the steps in the previous recipe and have set up SQL server to host the Management database on.

## How to do it...

The following list shows you the fundamental steps involved in this recipe and the tasks required to complete the recipe:

- Install the App-V 5 Server prerequisites
- Install the Management and Publishing server roles of App-V 5
- Install the latest App-V 5 hotfix

 App-V 5 on Windows Server 2012 R2 has few prerequisites compared to other editions of Windows Server. If running a previous version of Windows Server, consult the following link before proceeding further: http://technet. microsoft.com/en-us/library/jj713458.aspx.

The implementation of the preceding steps is as follows:

1. On the server APPV1, download and install the Microsoft Visual C++ 2013 Redistributable Package for both the x64 and x86 architectures from the following link: https://www.microsoft.com/en-us/download/details. aspx?id=40784.

2. Next, install the required Window Server features by executing the following command in a PowerShell session:

   ```
   Install-WindowsFeature -Name Web-Static-Content, Web-Default-Doc,
   Web-Asp-Net45, Web-Net-Ext45, Web-ISAPI-Ext, Web-ISAPI-Filter,
   Web-Windows-Auth, Web-Filtering -IncludeManagementTools -Restart
   ```

3. With the prerequisites installed, mount the MDOP 2014 R2 ISO file and navigate to `D: \App-V\App-V 5.0 SP3\Server`, where `D` is the drive letter of the mounted ISO file.

4. Launch the `appv_server_setup.exe` application to begin the installation process.

5. On the installation splash page, click on **Install**.

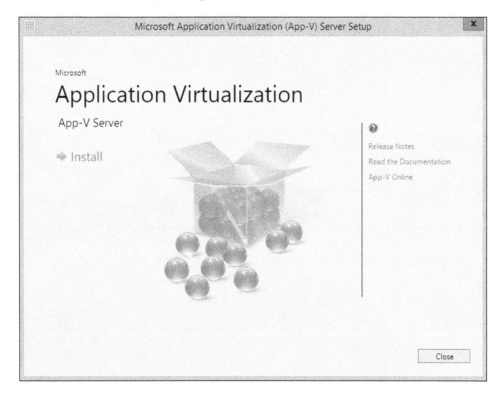

6. Review the **Software Licence Terms** and select the **I accept the license terms** radio button and click on **Next**.

7. Select the **Use Microsoft Update when I check for updates** radio box and click on **Next**.

8.  Select the **Management Server**, **Management Server DB** and **Publishing Server** features and click on **Next**.

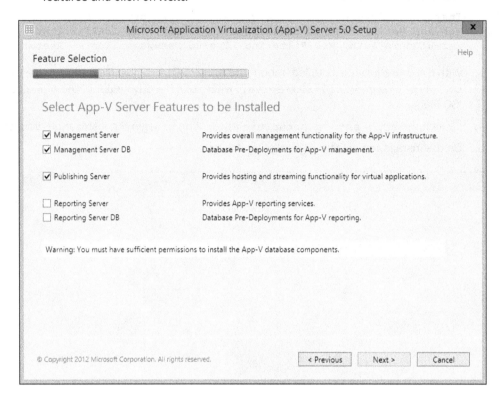

9.  Review the default installation location and click on **Next**.

10. On the **Create New Management Server Database** page, leave the **Use the default instance** and **Use the default configuration** radio boxes selected and click on **Next**.

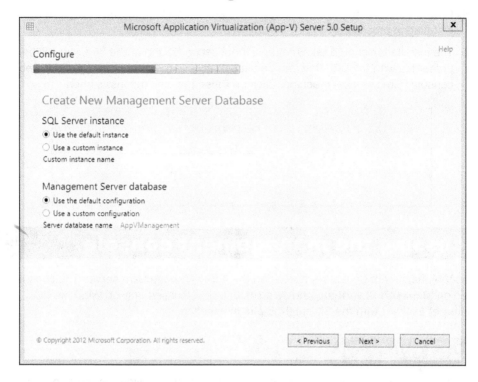

11. Review the **Create New Management Server Database** page and click on **Next**.

12. Set the **demo\App-V Administrators** security group as the group that is authorized to manage App-V and set **Port binding** to 440 (to match the firewall rule configured in the second recipe). Click on **Next**.

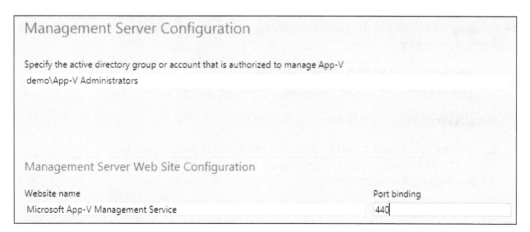

13. In the **Publishing Server configuration** option, set **Port binding** to 441 and leave all other settings as the defaults.

14. Review the list of the features to be installed and click on **Install** to begin the installation process.

15. The installation should take minutes, if not seconds, and at the end, you will be presented with the URL that can be used to access the App-V management web console from the local machine. Click on **Close** to finish the installation.

 App-V Server Setup has completed successfully

Next Steps

1 Access the management server web console at http://localhost:440/Console.html

# Accessing the management console

The App-V Management Console is hosted on the App-V Management server. The console is based on **Microsoft Silverlight**, and as such, can be accessed only on Windows PCs from Internet Explorer with the Silverlight 5 plugin installed.

## Getting ready

This recipe assumes that you have completed the steps in the previous recipe and have set up an App-V Management server with the Publishing role included. All of the actions in this task will be conducted on a domain-joined Windows 8.1 client.

## How to do it...

The following list shows you the fundamental steps involved in this recipe and the tasks required to complete the recipe:

  ▸   Install the latest version of Microsoft Silverlight

  ▸   Browse to the web-based management console and log in

The implementation of the preceding steps is as follows:

1. On your Windows 8.1 client, open Internet Explorer and browse to `http://www.microsoft.com/getsilverlight`. Then, click on the **Install Silverlight** button.

2. Allow the download to complete and then launch the **Install Silverlight** application and click on **Install now** to begin the installation. Close any open Internet Explorer windows.

3. Open Internet Explorer and browse to `http://appv1.demo.org:440/Console.html`.

4. A dialogue box will prompt you to log in with your credentials. Log in with the Sam Adams account created earlier, which is part of the App-V Administrators security group.

5. Once logged in, you will be presented with the Packages screen of the console. Note that the name of the account is listed in the top-right hand corner and that you can check the version number of the console by clicking on the **About** option.

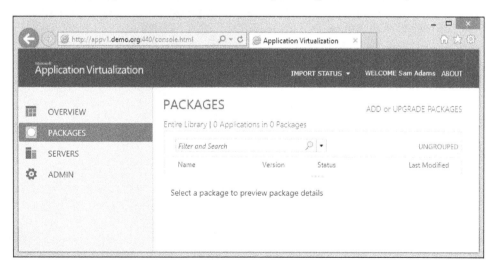

# Adding additional administrators

App-V leverages Active Directory Security Groups and user accounts to define administrators. When installing the App-V Management server, you can only choose a single Security Group or account; you can then configure extra accounts to manage your App-V deployment through the web-based management console.

## Getting ready

This recipe assumes that you have completed the steps in the previous recipe and have successfully logged in to the App-V management server.

## How to do it...

The following list shows you the fundamental steps involved in this recipe and the tasks required to complete the recipe:

▶ Add an Active Directory Security Group as an App-V administrator

▶ Add an Active Directory user account as an App-V administrator

▶ Remove administrator permissions from a Security Group or User account

The implementation of the preceding steps is as follows:

1. Log in to the App-V management console and select **Admin**. When the page refreshes, you will see the current administrators that are assigned to the App-V server. Click on **Add Administrator** in the top-right hand corner of the page.

2. In the **Active Directory Name** box, enter the name of the security group in the format `<domain>\<security group name>`. In this case, enter `demo\Domain Admins` and then click on **Check**.

3. Select the **demo\Domain Admins** security group from the drop-down menu that appears and click on **Add** to confirm the selection:

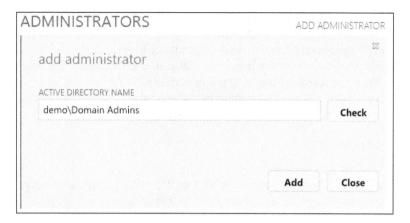

4. Alternatively, you can type the name of a user account again in the format `<domain>\<account name>`. In the following demonstration, you can see that the account user **Maddy** has been added and that its status as a user account instead of a security group is listed under the **Type** heading.

5. To remove a security group or user account from the administrators list, right-click on it and select the **remove as administrator** option.

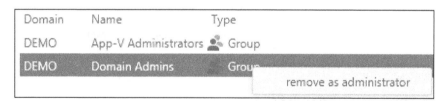

6. A confirmation dialogue will appear at the top of the page. Click on **Confirm** to complete the removal.

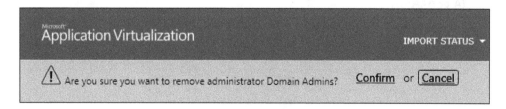

# Deploying a second Publishing server

The App-V Publishing server regularly polls and caches the list of App-V packages and applications to present to the clients. Deploying a second Publishing Server and utilizing NLB between the servers provides a basic level of redundancy to your clients, as well as offering a way to scale out your deployment in the event that your initial publishing server becomes overwhelmed. The App-V capacity planning guide at the following link can prove helpful in determining whether you will need an additional publishing server: `https://technet.microsoft.com/en-gb/library/dn595131.aspx`.

## Getting ready

This recipe assumes you have provisioned APPV1 as prescribed in the previous recipes and that you have provisioned APPV2 for use throughout this recipe.

## How to do it...

The following list shows you the fundamental steps involved in this recipe and the tasks required to complete the recipe:

- ▶ Create a DNS entry for use with the NLB cluster
- ▶ Install and configure NLB between APPV1 and APPV2
- ▶ Install the Publishing server role on APPV2
- ▶ Register the server in the App-V management console on APPV1
- ▶ Configure the Publishing Server website to accept requests from the NLB domain name

The implementation of the preceding steps is as follows:

1. On DC, launch the DNS management console, expand **Forward Lookup Zones**, and right-click on your domain. From the drop-down menu, select **New Host (A or AAAA)...**.

2.  Set the name as **app-vpublishing** and the **IP address** to **172.16.0.13**. Click on **Add Host** to create the record:

3.  On APPV1 and APPV2, run the following command in a PowerShell session to install the NLB feature:

```
Install-WindowsFeature -Name NLB -IncludeManagementTools -Restart
```

4.  Complete steps 5 to 16 of the *Internet information services configuration* recipe, setting up an NLB cluster between APPV1 and APPV2 with a cluster IP address of `172.16.0.13`, the **Full Internet** name of **app-vpublishing.demo.org** with **Multicast** as the **Cluster operation** mode.

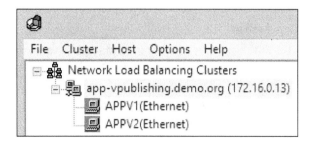

5. With the cluster configured being the installation process for App-V on the server APPV2 (as per the instructions given in the *Deploying a standalone management and publishing server* recipe), simply select the **Publishing Server** role from the **Select App-V Server Features to be Installed** page:

Select App-V Server Features to be Installed

| | |
|---|---|
| ☐ Management Server | Provides overall management functionality for the App-V infrastructure. |
| ☐ Management Server DB | Database Pre-Deployments for App-V management. |
| ☑ Publishing Server | Provides hosting and streaming functionality for virtual applications. |
| ☐ Reporting Server | Provides App-V reporting services. |
| ☐ Reporting Server DB | Database Pre-Deployments for App-V reporting. |

6. On the **Publishing Server Configuration** page, set **http://appv1.demo.org:440** as the management service to be used by this publishing server. In addition, set **441** as the **Port binding** for the **Publishing Server Web Site Configuration**:

Publishing Server Configuration

Specify the management service to be used by this publishing server

http://appv1.demo.org:440

Publishing Server Web Site Configuration

| Website name | Port binding |
|---|---|
| Microsoft App-V Publishing Service | 441 |

7. Complete the installation.

8. On your Windows 8.1 client machine, log in to the App-V web-based management console, and from the navigation bar on the right, select **Servers**.

9. Click on **Register New Server**. In the **Server Name** box that appears, enter the name of your second publishing server in the format `<domain>\<hostname of the server>`; In this example, **demo\APPV2**.

10. Click on the **Check** button and from the drop-down list that appears, select the server **demo\APPV2** and click on **Add** to include the server in the list of publishing servers.

 By default, the publishing server will poll the management server every 10 minutes for updates to the packages. You can force an update by restarting the **AppVPublishing Application Pool** service in the IIS management console. It is also possible to change the interval by modifying the registry on a publishing server. Visit `http://support.microsoft.com/kb/2780177` for more details.

11. To complete the configuration, open the IIS management console on APPV1, expand **Sites**, and select the **Microsoft App-V Publishing Service** website. On the **Actions** pane, select **Bindings...**.

12. Select the existing binding and click on **Edit...**.

13. Enter **app-vpublishing.demo.org** as your **Host name** and click on **OK**. Close the **Site Bindings** window.

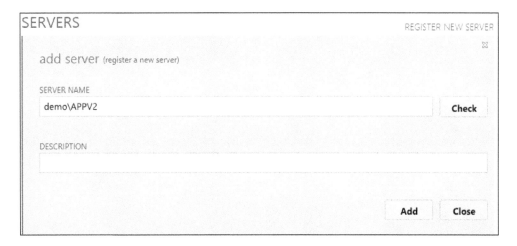

14. Repeat steps 11 to 13 for the server APPV2.

# 2

# Deploying App-V 5 Clients and Updates

In this chapter, we will cover:

- ▶ Obtaining the App-V 5 SP3 prerequisites
- ▶ Deploying client prerequisites through SCCM 2012 R2
- ▶ Deploying the App-V client through Group Policy
- ▶ Deploying the App-V client through SCCM 2012 R2
- ▶ Deploying App-V client updates through Group Policy
- ▶ Deploying App-V client updates through SCCM 2012 R2
- ▶ Deploying the App-V client UI through SCCM 2012
- ▶ Applying settings to the App-V client using Group Policy

# Introduction

The App-V 5 client is at the core of any App-V deployment, regardless of the method of deploying the applications onto the clients, whether via the publishing server, electronic software distribution, or **System Center Configuration Manager** (**SCCM**). In addition, the App-V client has a number of prerequisites that need to be in place prior to installation.

During the course of this chapter, we will be carrying out the steps on the DC, FS1, FS2, and SCCM servers and on our Windows 8.1 and Windows 7 client PCs (which will be used for testing purposes).

# Obtaining the App-V 5 SP3 prerequisites

This recipe shows you how to obtain the prerequisites for an App-V client installation on a Windows 8.1 or Windows 7 client PC.

## Getting ready

It is assumed that you have completed the tasks in the previous chapter and configured the DC, FS1, and FS2 servers. In addition, you should provision two client machines, one with Windows 8.1 installed and the other with Windows 7 SP1 installed.

## How to do it...

The following list shows you the high-level steps involved in this recipe and the tasks required to complete the recipe. (All of the actions in this recipe will take place on the servers with the hostnames DC and FS1. Note that FS2 must also be running to allow for DFS replication between the hosts.)

1. Download the prerequisite installers and store them in a set of subfolders.

2. On the server FS1, build a folder structure as per the following image. Note that the files are contained within the path to the FileStore DFS namespace that was created in the previous chapter.

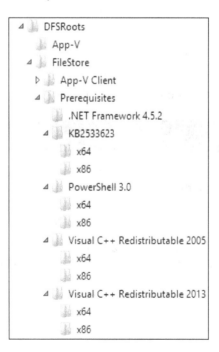

These folders will be accessible from `\\demo.org\filestore\`.

3. Download the prerequisites (for an up-to-date list, visit `http://technet.microsoft.com/en-us/library/dn858705.aspx`) and store them in the folders created in the previous step, making sure to separate out the 32-bit and 64-bit editions.

 At the time of writing, .NET Framework 4.5.2 was the latest supported version. For deployment through Group Policy/SCCM, you must use the offline installer, which can be downloaded from `http://www.microsoft.com/en-us/download/details.aspx?id=42642`.

Although not mentioned on the App-V 5 SP3 documentation, Visual C++ Redistributable 2005 is also a requirement. The relevant version can be downloaded from `http://www.microsoft.com/en-us/download/details.aspx?id=26347`.

Finally, update KB2533623 for Windows 7 computers is available through Windows Update. If your computers are using Windows Update with the default settings, it is likely that this update is already deployed on your machines.

# Deploying client prerequisites through SCCM 2012 R2

This recipe shows you how to deploy the prerequisites for an App-V client installation on a Windows 8.1 or Windows 7 client PC using System Centre Configuration Manager 2012 R2.

## Getting ready

It is assumed that you have completed the steps in the previous chapter and configured the servers DC, FS1 and FS2. In addition, you should provision a SCCM server; the configuration of this server is outside the scope of this book. We will also be using fresh Windows 8.1 and Windows 7 SP1 clients that do not already have the prerequisites installed.

 For information on deploying Microsoft SCCM, visit TechNet at `https://technet.microsoft.com/en-us/library/gg682129.aspx`.

## How to do it...

The following list shows you the high-level steps involved in this recipe and the tasks required to complete the recipe (all of the actions in this recipe will take place on the server with the hostname SCCM):

- ▸ Create a device group for the SCCM clients.
- ▸ Create and deploy a .NET Framework 4.5.2 package.
- ▸ Create and deploy a KB2533623 package.
- ▸ Create and deploy a PowerShell 3.0 package.
- ▸ Create and deploy a Visual C++ Redistributable 2005 package.
- ▸ Create and deploy a Visual C++ Redistributable 2013 package.

The implementation of the preceding tasks is as follows:

1. On your SCCM server, browse to **Assets and Compliance**, right-click on **Device Collections**, and then click on **Create Device Collection**.

2. Give the collection the name `App-V 5 Deployment`, set the limiting collection to **All Systems**, then click on **Next**.

3. Define membership rules as required for your deployment and click on **Next**.

4. Review the summary and click on **Next**. Finally, click on **Close** to complete the wizard.

5. Browse to **Software Library | Application Management** and right-click on **Packages**. From the menu that appears, select **Folder** and then click on **Create Folder**.

6. Give the folder the name `App-V 5 Prerequisites` and click on **OK**.

7. To deploy the .NET Framework, right-click on the `App-V 5 Prerequisites` folder you just created and click on **Create Package**.

8. In the window that appears, set the name as `.NET Framework`, and enter `Microsoft` in the **Manufacturer** field and `4.5.2` in the **Version** field. Tick the **This package contains source files** check box, set the source folder to `\\demo.org\filestore\Prerequisites\.NET Framework 4.5.2`, and click on **Next**.

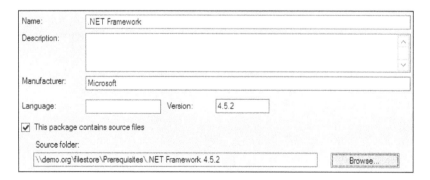

9. Leave **Standard program** selected and click on **Next**.

10. Set the name of the standard program to `Install`, set the command line to `NDP452-KB2901907-x86-x64-AllOS-ENU.exe /q /norestart`, and set the program to **Only run when no user is logged on**; leave all the other settings to their defaults and click on **Next**.

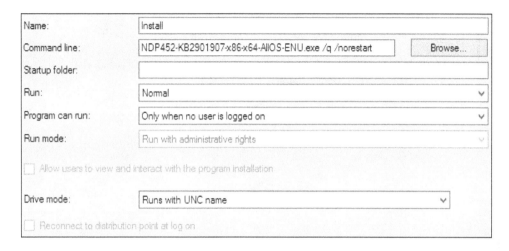

11. On the requirements screen, leave the defaults set and click on **Next** to go to the summary screen. Again, click on **Next** for the wizard to create the package. Click on **Close** to finish the wizard.

12. Right-click on the .NET Framework package you just created, and on the menu that appears, click on **Distribute Content**.

13. In the window that appears, click on **Next**.

14. Add the package to your distribution points and click on **Next**.

15. Review the summary and click on **Next** through to the completion screen. Click on **Close** to finish the wizard.

16. Right-click on the .NET Framework package and click on **Deploy**.

17. Set the **App-V 5 Deployment** device group that you created earlier as the collection for the deployment and click on **Next**.

18. Review the content screen and click on **Next**.

19. Set **Purpose** to **Required** and click on **Next**.

20. Set a deployment schedule and click on **Next**.

21. Review the **user experience and distribution points** screens and click on **Next**.

22. Review the summary and click on **Next** to begin the deployment, clicking on **Close** once the deployment has started.

23. To deploy KB2533623, follow steps 7-22 of this recipe, setting the program names as KB2533623 - x86 and KB2533623 - x64 with the folder paths respectively as follows:

   ❑ `\\demo.org\filestore\Prerequisites\KB2533623\x86`

   ❑ `\\demo.org\filestore\Prerequisites\KB2533623\x64`

 Use the commands `wusa.exe Windows6.1-KB2533623-x86.msu /quiet /norestart` and `wusa.exe Windows6.1-KB2533623-x64.msu /quiet /norestart` as the command-line paths.

| Name: | KB2533623 - x86 |
|---|---|
| Description: | |
| Manufacturer: | Microsoft| |
| Language: | Version: |

☑ This package contains source files

Source folder:

`\\demo.org\filestore\Prerequisites\KB2533623\x86`     Browse...

24. In addition, on the requirements screen, select **This program can only run on specified platforms** and tick **All Windows 7 (32-bit)** or **All Windows 7 (64-bit)**, depending on the operating system architecture that the update is being deployed to.

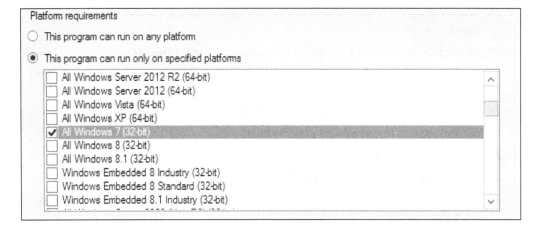

Platform requirements

○ This program can run on any platform

◉ This program can run only on specified platforms

- ☐ All Windows Server 2012 R2 (64-bit)
- ☐ All Windows Server 2012 (64-bit)
- ☐ All Windows Vista (64-bit)
- ☐ All Windows XP (64-bit)
- ☑ All Windows 7 (32-bit)
- ☐ All Windows 8 (32-bit)
- ☐ All Windows 8.1 (32-bit)
- ☐ Windows Embedded 8 Industry (32-bit)
- ☐ Windows Embedded 8 Standard (32-bit)
- ☐ Windows Embedded 8.1 Industry (32-bit)

25. To deploy PowerShell 3.0, repeat steps 7-23 of this recipe, setting the program names as PowerShell - x86 and PowerShell - x64 with Microsoft as manufacturer, 3.0 as version, and the folder paths respectively as follows:

    ❑ `\\demo.org\filestore\Prerequisites\PowerShell 3.0\x86`

    ❑ `\\demo.org\filestore\Prerequisites\PowerShell 3.0\x64`

 Use `wusa.exe Windows6.1-KB2506143-x86.msu /quiet / norestart` and `wusa.exe Windows6.1-KB2506143-x64.msu /quiet /norestart` as the command-line paths.

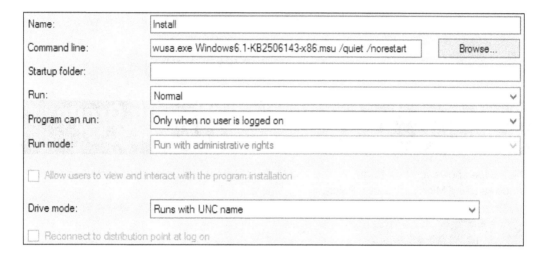

| Name: | Install | |
|---|---|---|
| Command line: | wusa.exe Windows6.1-KB2506143-x86.msu /quiet /norestart | Browse... |
| Startup folder: | | |
| Run: | Normal | ⌄ |
| Program can run: | Only when no user is logged on | ⌄ |
| Run mode: | Run with administrative rights | ⌄ |
| ☐ Allow users to view and interact with the program installation | | |
| Drive mode: | Runs with UNC name | ⌄ |
| ☐ Reconnect to distribution point at log on | | |

26. To deploy Visual C++ Redistributable 2005, follow steps 7-23 of this recipe. Follow the same naming and folder path sequences as the other packages, but use `vcredist_x86.exe /q` and `vcredist_x64.exe /q` as the command-line paths instead.

27. Finally, to deploy Visual C++ Redistributable 2013, again follow steps 7-23 of this recipe. Again, use the same naming and folder path sequence; however, in a slight deviation from the previous steps, use `vcredist_x86.exe /q /norestart` and `vcredist_x64.exe /q /norestart` as the command-line paths.

28. You should now have 8 packages deployed to your clients, as per the following screenshot:

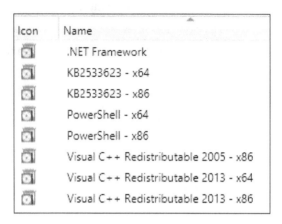

| Icon | Name |
|---|---|
| | .NET Framework |
| | KB2533623 - x64 |
| | KB2533623 - x86 |
| | PowerShell - x64 |
| | PowerShell - x86 |
| | Visual C++ Redistributable 2005 - x86 |
| | Visual C++ Redistributable 2013 - x64 |
| | Visual C++ Redistributable 2013 - x86 |

# Deploying the App-V client through Group Policy

This recipe shows you how to deploy the App-V client installation on any supported edition of Windows using Microsoft Group Policy.

## Getting ready

It is assumed that you have completed the tasks in the previous chapter and configured the servers DC, FS1, and FS2. In addition, it assumed you have installed the client prerequisites on your testing machines.

## How to do it...

The following list shows you the high-level steps involved in this recipe and the tasks required to complete the recipe. (All of the actions in this recipe will take place on the servers with the hostnames DC and FS1. Note that FS2 must also be running to allow for DFS replication between the hosts.)

▶ Extract the App-V 5 **Microsoft Scripted Installer** (**MSI**).

▶ Obtain **Windows Install Transform** (.MST) to be used with the installer.

▶ Publish the MSI using Group Policy to your clients.

The implementation of the preceding tasks is as follows:

1.  Create the following folder structure on `FS1` to host the App-V client installers:

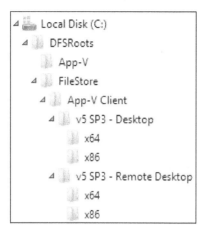

2.  Copy and paste the `appv_client_setup.exe` application into the `v5 SP3 - Desktop` folder.

3.  Remaining within the folder, press and hold the *Shift* key on your keyboard and right-click on the whitespace. From the menu that appears, click on **Open command window here**.

4.  Enter the following command to extract the installation files into this folder:

    **`appv_client_setup /layout`**

5.  Cut and paste the `appv_client_MSI_x86.msi` installer into the `x86` subfolder and the `appv_client_MSI_x64.msi` installer into the `x64` subfolder. You may delete the `EULA` folder that has been created along with the `appv_client_setup.exe` application.

> The App-V installer requires the `AcceptEULA=1` property to be set during installation; however, Group Policy software deployment does not include the features necessary to set this property. Using the free Ocra MSI editor, it is possible to create a transform file which will add this property into the MSI, you can learn how to install the Ocra editor at `http://myworldofit.net/?p=1368`.

6. Open your web browser and navigate to `http://myworldofit.net/?dl_id=28`, download the ZIP file presented, and copy the `AcceptEULA.mst` file into the folder containing the MSI file for the App-V installers.

| DFSRoots ▸ FileStore ▸ App-V Client ▸ v5 SP3 - Desktop ▸ x86 | | ∨ ⟳ | Search x86 |
|---|---|---|---|
| Name ▲ | Date modified | Type | Size |
| ▢ AcceptEULA.mst | 21/12/2014 22:55 | MST File | 20 KB |
| 🗃 appv_client_MSI_x86 | 30/10/2014 21:32 | Windows Installer ... | 9,024 KB |

7. On the server `DC`, open the **Group Policy Management Console**, expand the tree structure, right-click on the Organizational Unit that contains your testing clients, and click on **Create new GPO in this domain, and link here it here....**

8. In the window that appears, set **App-V 5 Installer** as the name of the new policy and click on **OK**.

9. Right-click on the policy that you just created and click on **Edit....**

10. In the window that appears, right-click on the policy and click on **Properties**. In the window that appears next, tick the checkbox next to **Disable User Configuration settings**, accepting any prompts that appear, and click on **OK** to close this window.

11. Expand **Computer Configuration | Policies | Software Settings** and right-click on **Software installation**. On the menu that appears, select **New** and then click on **Package....**

12. In the file picker that appears, browse to `\\demo.org\filestore\App-V Client\v5 SP3 - Desktop\x64` and select the MSI presented.

13. In the new window that appears, select the **Advanced** option and click on **OK**.

14. In the new window that appears, select the **Modifications** tab and click on **Add....**

15. In the file picker that appears, select the `AcceptEULA.mst` file and click on **Open**.

16. Repeat steps 11-15 of this recipe for the x86 installer, adding the installer to the same Group Policy object. In addition, after applying the .mst file to the installer, navigate to the **Deployment** tab and click on **Advanced...**.

17. In the window that appears, remove the mark from the checkbox next to **Make this 32-bit X86 application available to Win64 machines** to prevent deploying the 32-bit version of the installer to 64-bit machines.

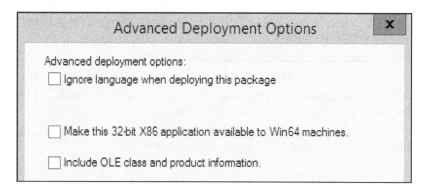

# Deploying the App-V client through SCCM 2012 R2

This recipe shows you how to deploy the App-V client installation on any supported edition of Windows using Microsoft System Centre Configuration Manager 2012 R2.

## Getting ready

It is assumed that you have completed the steps in the previous chapter and configured the servers DC, FS1, and FS2. In addition, it is assumed that you have installed the client prerequisites on your testing machines. Finally, this recipe uses the extracted installers and folder structure created in steps 1-5 of the previous recipe.

## How to do it...

The following list shows you the high-level steps involved in this recipe and the tasks required to complete the recipe (all of the actions in this recipe will take place on the server with the hostname SCCM):

  ▸ Create an App-V application.

  ▸ Distribute the application and publish to clients.

The implementation of the preceding tasks is as follows:

1. On your SCCM server, browse to **Software Library** and expand **Application Management**. Right-click on **Applications**, select **Folder**, and click on **Create Folder**.

2. In the window that appears, set the name of the folder to **App-V 5 Client**. Right-click on the newly created folder and click on **Create Application**.

3. Set **Type of the application** to **Windows Installer** and the file path to \\demo.org\ filestore\App-V Client\v5 SP3 - Desktop\x64\appv_client_MSI_ x64.msi and click on **Next**.

4. Review the imported information and click on **Next**.

5. On the **general information** screen, add AcceptEULA=1 at the end of the **Installation program** as shown in the following screenshot, leave all the other settings at their default values, and click on **Next**.

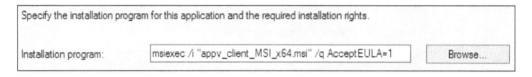

6. Review the summary screen and click on **Next**. Once the wizard is complete, click on **Close** to finish.

7. With the application that you just created, click the **Deployment Types** tab at the bottom of the screen, right-click on the deployment type shown and click on **Properties**.

8. In the window that appears, navigate to the **Requirements** tab and click on **Add...**.

9. In the **Create Requirement** window that appears, set **Category** to **Device** and **Condition** to **Operating system** with **Rule type** set to **Value** and **Operator** to **One of**. Put checkmarks next to the **All Windows 7 (64-bit)**, **All Windows 8 (64-bit)**, and **All Windows 8.1 (64-bit)** options that appear, clicking **OK** once done. Close any open windows and return to the SCCM management console.

10. Distribute the application to your distribution point by right-clicking on the application and selecting **Distribute Content** from the drop-down menu. Click on **Next** through the general and content screens, add your SCCM server to the content destination, and continue through the wizard.

11. Finally, to deploy the App-V client to your machines, right-click on the application and click on **Deploy** on the menu that appears.

12. In the new window, set **Collection** to **App-V 5 Deployment** and click on **Next**.

13. Review the content screen, ensuring that the application has been distributed, and click on **Next**.

14. On the **Deployment Settings** screen, set **Purpose** to **Required** and click on **Next**.

15. Review the **Scheduling** and **User Experience** screens and click on **Next**.

To prevent the end user from being interrupted with a message stating that the App-V client is being installed, set the user notifications option on the user experience screen to **Hide in Software Centre and all notifications**.

16. Review the alerts and summary screens, clicking **Next** as you go, until the completion of the wizard and click on **Close**.

# Deploying App-V client updates through Group Policy

This recipe will show you how to apply a hotfix to the App-V installer and deploy it to your clients with Group Policy.

App-V updates are released as cumulative hotfixes for specific issues. Special care should be taken to thoroughly test updates before they are released into your production environment as a misconfiguration can easily render the App-V client inoperable.

## Getting ready

It is assumed that you have installed the App-V client on a Windows 8.1 client.

In addition, you should download the latest App-V hotfix; the latest information on App-V hotfixes can be found on the App-V team blog at `http://blogs.technet.com/b/appv/`. This example will use App-V 5 SP3 Hotfix 2, which is listed under Microsoft KB3060458.

## How to do it...

The following list shows you the high-level steps involved in this recipe and the tasks required to complete the recipe. (All of the actions in this recipe will take place on servers with the hostnames `DC` and `FS1`. Note that `FS2` must also be running to allow for DFS replication between the hosts.)

- ▸ Obtain and extract the latest App-V hotfix.
- ▸ Apply the hotfix to your App-V installer.
- ▸ Publish the updated MSI to your clients by using Group Policy.

The implementation of the preceding tasks is as follows:

1. With the downloaded hotfix in an easy-to-access folder, double-click on it to bring up Microsoft Self-Extractor. When prompted, click on **Continue** to begin the extraction, setting the folder to extract the files to `C:\Temp`.

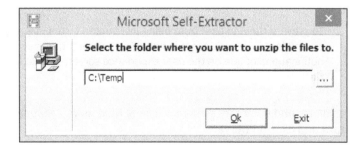

2. Once the files have been extracted, click on **OK** to close.

3. Navigate to `C:\Temp` and note that you have two applications, which can be used to update the Desktop Client (`AppV5.0SP3_Client_KB3039022.exe`) and RDS (`AppV5.0SP3_RDS_KB3039022.exe`) versions of App-V along with a text file. Press and hold the *Shift* key on your keyboard, right-click on the whitespace, and click on **Open command window here**.

4. With the command window open, run the command `AppV5.0SP3_Client_KB3039022 /layout`, which will in turn generate a further application (`appv_client_setup_patch.exe`), two Windows installer patches (`appv_client_kb3039022_x86.msp` and `appv_client_kb3039022_x64.msp`), and a folder called `EULA`.

5. To update the 64-bit App-V installer, copy `appv_client_MSI_x64.msi` from `\\demo.org\filestore\App-V Client\v5 SP3 - Desktop\x64` into `C:\Temp`, after which you will have a folder that looks similar to the one in the following screenshot.

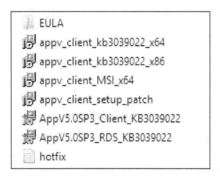

6. Within `C:\Temp`, press and hold the *Shift* key and right-click on the whitespace; select **Open command window here**.

7. To apply the hotfix to the App-V installer, enter the command `msiexec /p appv_client_kb3060458_x64.msp /a appv_client_MSI_x64.msi`. This command calls **msiexec**, instructs it to use `appv_client_kb3060458_x64.msp` as the patch (with the `/p` switch) and to apply it to an administrative installation (with the `/a` switch) of the App-V installer with the filename `appv_client_MSI_x64.msi`.

8.  Once the application of the hotfix is complete, you will note that the timestamp on the App-V installer has been updated and that a folder called `Microsoft Application Virtualization` has been created (this folder can be ignored). Copy and paste the updated App-V installer to `\\demo.org\filestore\App-V Client\v5 SP3 HF2 - Desktop\x64`. In addition, copy and paste the `AcceptEULA.mst` transform file into the folder that you downloaded in the third recipe of this chapter. Once complete, you will have a folder that looks like the following screenshot:

9.  On the server `DC`, launch the Group Policy Management Console, expand **demo.org | Domain Computers**, and right-click on the **App-V 5 Installer** GPO that you created earlier. Click on **Edit...**.

10. In the window that appears, expand **Computer Configuration | Policies | Software Settings**, right-click on **Software installation**, and go to **New | Package...**.

11. In the window that appears, navigate to the updated App-V installer at `\\demo.org\filestore\App-V Client\v5 SP3 HF2 - Desktop\x64\appv_client_MSI_x64.msi`, select it, and click on **Open**.

12. The **Deploy Software** window will open. Select the **Advanced** radio button and click on **OK**.

13. In the window that appears, go to the **General** tab and append the name of the package with `v5 SP3 HF2` to denote the new version.

14. In the **Upgrades** tab, click on **Add...**.

15. In the window that appears, select **Choose a package from Current Group Policy Object (GPO)** and select the 64-bit App-V client package that you created in the recipe, *Deploying the App-V client through Group Policy*, in this chapter. Be sure to select the **Package can upgrade over the existing package** radio button and click on **OK**.

 Selecting **Uninstall the existing package** and then installing the upgrade package can prevent the App-V client from functioning after the installation. As mentioned earlier, be sure to test any App-V package updates before rolling them out to your production environment.

16. On the **Modifications** tab, click on **Add...**.

17. In the window that appears, select the `AcceptEULA.mst` file and click on **Open**.

18. Finally, click on **OK** to begin deploying the update to your clients.

19. Repeat steps 1-18 of this recipe for the x 86 installer, adding the installer to the same Group Policy object. In addition, after applying the `.mst` file to the installer, navigate to the **Deployment** tab and click on **Advanced...**.

20. In the window that appears, remove the mark from the checkbox next to **Make this 32-bit X86 application available to Win64 machines** to prevent deploying the 32-bit version of the installer to 64-bit machines.

# Deploying App-V client updates through SCCM 2012 R2

This recipe will show you how to deploy App-V client updates through Microsoft SCCM. A key advantage of SCCM over Group Policy deployment is that you do not need to combine the hotfix with the original App-V installer to deploy the update.

## Getting ready

It is assumed that you have installed the App-V client installed on a Windows 8.1 client.

In addition, you should download the latest App-V hotfix; the latest information on App-V hotfixes can be found on the App-V team blog at `http://blogs.technet.com/b/appv/`. This example will use App-V 5 SP3 Hotfix 2, which is listed under Microsoft KB3060458.

## How to do it...

The following list shows you the high-level steps involved in this recipe and the tasks required to complete the recipe (all of the actions in this recipe will take place on the server with the hostname SCCM):

► Obtain and extract the latest App-V hotfix.

► Publish the update package to your clients by using SCCM.

The implementation of the preceding tasks is as follows:

1. With the downloaded hotfix in an easy-to-access folder, double-click on it to bring up Microsoft Self-Extractor. When prompted, click on **Continue** to begin the extraction, setting `C:\Temp` as the location to extract the files to.

2. Once the files have been extracted, click on **OK** to close.

3. Navigate to C:\Temp and note that you have two applications, which can be used to update the Desktop Client (AppV5.0SP3_Client_KB3039022.exe) and RDS (AppV5.0SP3_RDS_KB3039022.exe) versions of App-V along with a text file. Press and hold the *Shift* key on your keyboard, right-click on the whitespace, and click on **Open command window here**.

4. With the command window open, run the command AppV5.0SP3_Client_ KB3039022 /layout, which will, in turn, generate a further application (appv_ client_setup_patch.exe), two Windows installer patches (appv_client_ kb3039022_x86.msp and appv_client_kb3039022_x64.msp) and a folder called EULA.

5. To update the 64-bit App-V client, copy appv_client_kb3039022_x64.msp to \\demo.org\filestore\App-V Client\v5 SP3 HF2 Standalone - Desktop\x64\.

6. On your SCCM server, browse to **Software Library** and expand **Application Management**. Right-click on **Packages**, select **Folder**, and click on **Create Folder**.

7. In the window that appears, set the name of the folder to App-V 5 Update. Right-click on the newly created folder and click on **Create Package**.

8. In the **Create Package and Program** wizard, set v5 SP3 HF2 x64 as the name and **Microsoft** as the **Manufacturer**. Tick the **This package contains source files** option and click on **Browse....**.

9. In the window that appears, keep **Source folder location** set to **Network path (UNC name)** and set **Source folder** to \\demo.org\filestore\App-V Client\v5 SP3 HF2 Standalone - Desktop\x64. Click on **OK** and then click on **Next** to advance to the next step of the wizard.

10. At the **Program Type** screen, leave **Standard program** selected and click on **Next**.

11. At the **Standard Program** screen, set **Name** to Install App-V v5 SP3 HF2 Update, **Command line** to msiexec /p appv_client_kb3039022_x64.msp /q, and **Program can run** to **Only when no user is logged on**. Click on **Next**.

This command calls msiexec to install the update with the /p switch, after which the file which is used to perform the update is mentioned (in this case, appv_client_kb3039002_x64.msp); finally, the /q switch is used to instruct the installer to run quietly. Note that the installer will require a reboot after completion; the installer is therefore set to run when no one is logged in, to prevent a user from being forcibly logged off mid-work.

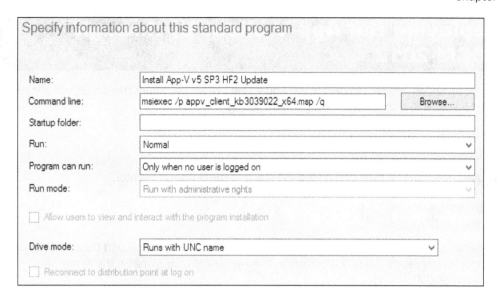

12. At the requirements screen, select the **This program can run only the specified platforms** radio button and place ticks in the **All Windows 7 (64-bit)**, **All Windows 8 (64-bit)**, and **All Windows 8.1 (64-bit)** checkboxes. Click on **Next**.

13. Review the summary screen and click on **Next**. Finally, click on **Close** to complete the wizard.

14. Right-click on the v5 SP3 HF2 x64 package you just created, and, on the menu that appears, click on **Distribute Content**.

15. In the window that appears, click on **Next**.

16. Add the package to your distribution points and click on **Next**.

17. Review the summary and click on **Next** through to the completion screen; then, click on **Close** to finish the wizard.

18. Right-click on the v5 SP3 HF2 x64 package and click on **Deploy**.

19. Set the **App-V 5 Deployment** device group that you created earlier as the collection for the deployment and click on **Next**.

20. Review the content screen and click on **Next**.

21. Set **Purpose** to **Required** and click on **Next**.

22. Set a deployment schedule and click on **Next**.

23. Review the **user experience and distribution points** screens and click on **Next**.

24. Review the **summary** screen and click on **Next** to begin the deployment, clicking **Close** once the deployment has started.

# Deploying the App-V client UI through SCCM 2012

This recipe shows you how to deploy the App-V client UI on any supported edition of Windows using Microsoft System Centre Configuration Manager 2012 R2.

## Getting ready

It is assumed that you have completed the steps in the previous chapter.

## How to do it...

The following list shows you the high-level steps involved in this recipe and the tasks required to complete the recipe (all of the actions in this recipe will take place on the server with the hostname SCCM):

- ▶ Download the App-V Client UI.
- ▶ Create an App-V Client UI application.
- ▶ Distribute the application and publish to clients.

The implementation of the preceding tasks is as follows:

1. Open your web browser and navigate to `http://www.microsoft.com/en-gb/download/details.aspx?id=41186`, download the `appv_client_ui_setup.msi` file, and store it on your DFS namespace in `\\demo.org\filestore\App-V Client UI`.

 Note that it is also possible to obtain an App-V package version of the Client UI, which can be extracted and deployed like any other App-V application.

2. Within the System Centre Management Console, navigate to **Software Library | Application Management | Applications**, right-click on the **App-V 5 Client** folder you created earlier, and click on **Create Application**.

3. In the new window that appears, accept the default type as **Windows Installer** and set the location to the path of the `appv_client_ui_setup.msi` file that you downloaded in the previous recipe.

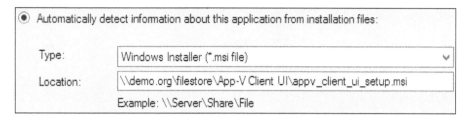

Automatically detect information about this application from installation files:

| Type: | Windows Installer (*.msi file) |
|---|---|
| Location: | \\demo.org\filestore\App-V Client UI\appv_client_ui_setup.msi |
| | Example: \\Server\Share\File |

4. Review the **import information** screen and click on **Next**.

5. At the **general information** screen, set **Installation Program** to `msiexec /i "appv_client_ui_setup.msi" /q ACCEPTEULA=1`, leaving all of the other settings to their default values, and click on **Next**.

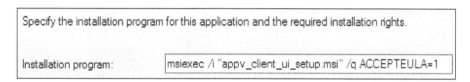

Specify the installation program for this application and the required installation rights.

| Installation program: | msiexec /i "appv_client_ui_setup.msi" /q ACCEPTEULA=1 |
|---|---|

6. Review the summary screen and click on **Next**. Finally, review the completion screen and click on **Close** to finish the wizard.

7. To distribute the application, right-click on the **Microsoft App-V 5.0 Client UI** application you just added and click on **Distribute Content** from the drop-down menu.

8. Review the general and content screens, clicking **Next** as you go to get to the content destination screen; add your SCCM distribution point to the content destination list; and click on **Next** to proceed.

9. Review the summary screen, clicking **Next** before reaching the completion screen. Click on **Close** to finish this wizard.

10. Finally, to deploy the client UI, right-click on its application and click on **Deploy**.

11. Set the **App-V 5 Deployment** device group as the collection and click on **Next**.

12. Review the content screen and click on **Next**.

13. At the deployment settings screen, set **Purpose** to **Required** to mandate that the software be deployed to PCs (instead of giving the end users an option) and click on **Next**.

14. Review the **scheduling**, **user experience**, **alerts**, and **summary** screens, clicking **Next** to proceed to the end of the wizard, and clicking on **Close** to finish.

15. According to your software deployment rules, the App-V Client UI will now be deployed to your PCs. Once installed, you can find it in the **Start** menu under **Programs** and listed as **Microsoft App-V 5.0 Client UI**.

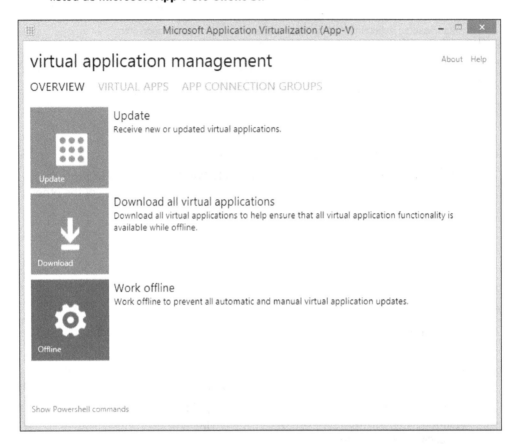

# Applying settings to the App-V client using Group Policy

Features of the App-V client can be centrally managed through Group Policy; this method of management is a particularly useful way of assigning the publishing servers that the client should contact to retrieve lists of applications to present to the user.

## Getting ready

It is assumed that you have completed the steps in the previous chapter. In addition, you should create a central store for Group Policy objects within your domain; a guide to how to create this store can be found at http://support.microsoft.com/kb/929841.

The Group Policy Central Store is a single location for the storage of Group Policy ADMX templates that ensures administrators are always working from a single set of policies.

## How to do it...

The following list shows you the high-level steps involved in this recipe and the tasks required to complete the recipe (all of the actions in this recipe will take place on the server with the hostname `DC`):

- Download the Microsoft Desktop Optimization Pack Group Policy Administrative templates and import them into the central store.
- Create a Group Policy object for your App-V settings and configure common settings.

The implementation of the preceding tasks is as follows:

1. Open your web browser and navigate to `http://www.microsoft.com/en-us/download/details.aspx?id=41183`. Download and run the `MDOP_ADMX_Templates.exe` file to extract the contents into your `downloads` folder.

2. Navigate to your downloads folder, open the `Microsoft Desktop Optimization Pack` folder, and copy the contents of the `App-V5.0SP3` folder (including all subfolders) into your central store.

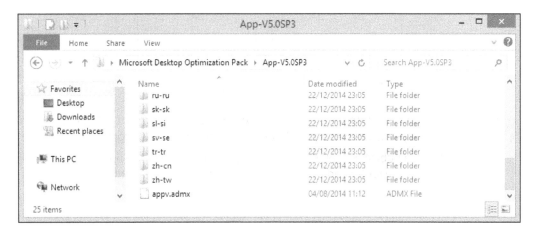

3. On the server `DC`, launch the Group Policy management console and expand the tree structure to show **Domain Computers**.

4. Right-click on **Domain Computers OU** and select **Create a GPO in this domain, and Link it here...**.

5. Set the name of the GPO to `App-V 5 Settings`.

6.  Right-click on the newly created policy and click on **Edit....**

7.  In the window that appears, right-click on the policy and select **Properties**.

8.  Place a mark in the checkbox next to **Disable User Configuration settings**, accept any information dialogs, and click on **OK**.

9.  Expand **Computer Configuration | Administrative Templates | System | App-V** to display the App-V policies.

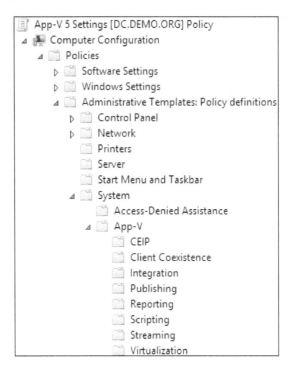

10. To configure the customer experience improvement program, head to the CEIP policy; disabling the policy will prevent CEIP data from being sent to Microsoft.

11. To configure a publishing server for the client to retrieve a list of applications, head to the **Publishing** folder and edit the policy settings on the **Publishing Server 1 Settings** item.

12. Enable the policy, setting **Publishing Server Display Name** to **app-vpublishing** and **Publishing Server URL** to **http://app-vpublishing.demo.org:441**.

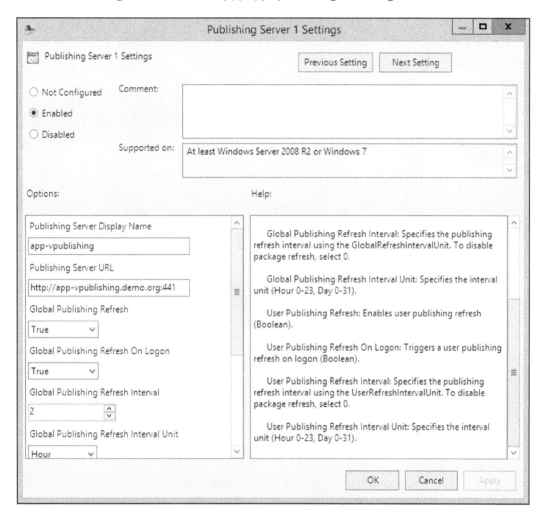

13. Continue to configure the settings by setting **Global Publishing Refresh** and **Global Publishing Refresh On Logon** to **True**, with a **Publishing Refresh Interval** setting of **2** and **Interval Unit** set to **Hour** (this will refresh the machine policy at the time of user logon and every 2 hours).

14. Finally, set **User Publishing Refresh** and **User Publishing Refresh on Logon** to **True** and the interval to **2 hours** as well (this will refresh the machine policy at the time of user logon and every 2 hours).

# 3
# Sequencing Applications

In this chapter, we will cover:

- ▶ Setting up the sequencer
- ▶ Sequencing Audacity sound editor
- ▶ Sequencing an Internet Explorer shortcut
- ▶ Sequencing an application hosted on a network share
- ▶ Dissecting an App-V 5 package
- ▶ Scripting in App-V 5

## Introduction

Sequencing an application captures the files, registry entries, shell extensions, services, shortcuts, and file extensions to be included in the virtual application package.

[  Note that device drivers cannot be virtualized and must be installed using traditional methods. Of particular note are printer capture drivers for software such as Microsoft OneNote and SMART Notebook. ]

Regardless of the method of deploying an App-V application, the sequencing process is the same; however, there are three different types of sequences that can be run per the following table:

 ▸ **Standard application**: This is the most common type and covers programs such as Audacity or Office365.

 ▸ **Add-on or Plug-in**: This covers extensions for standard applications, for example, the Lame MP3 extension in Audacity or an automation plug-in for Microsoft Excel.

 ▸ **Middleware**: This covers prerequisites for standard applications, for example, the Java extension.

Back in 2012, Microsoft produced the App-V 5.0 Sequencing Guide; although some elements of this guide are now out of date, many of the concepts and in-depth technical information is still valid. This guide can be downloaded from `http://www.microsoft.com/en-us/download/details.aspx?id=27760`.

# Setting up the sequencer

This recipe shows you how to set up a sequencing client on a Windows 8.1 virtual machine. Unless there are particular hardware requirements to capture an application (for example, a 3D program that requires access to hardware acceleration), you should use a virtual machine to run the sequencer. Doing so allows you to take snapshots of the process as you go, to allow you to quickly go back to a point in time in the event that the capture did not happen as expected.

Finally, it's worth noting that your App-V sequencer should be running the same operating system version with the same libraries (like the .NET Framework) installed. Doing so aids any troubleshooting processes in the event that an application doesn't run as expected.

## Getting ready

To complete these steps, you will need Windows 8.1 installed on a virtual machine.

## How to do it...

The following list shows you the high-level steps involved in this recipe and the tasks required to complete the recipe (all of the actions in this recipe will take place on the sequencing client called `WIN8SEQUENCER`):

 ▸ Download and install all Windows updates.

 ▸ Install the App-V sequencer.

The implementation of the preceding tasks is as follows:

1. Create a snapshot of the virtual machine.
2. On WIN8SEQUENCER, run Windows Update and install all available updates.
3. Begin the installation of the App-V sequencer; the installation file can be found on the `App-V 5 SP3 ISO` under `APP-V SEQUENCER 5.0 SP3`.

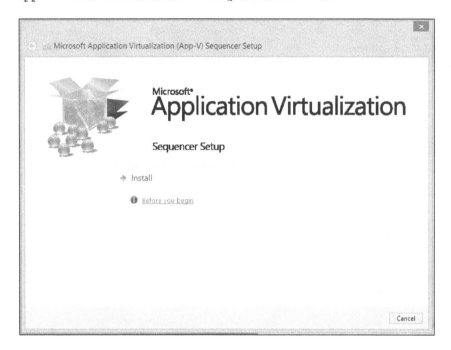

4. Click on **Install**, review the software license terms, select the **I accept the license terms** radio button, and then click on **Next**.
5. Select the **Join the Customer Experience Improvement Program** radio button and click on **Install**.
6. Accept any **User Account Control** popups by selecting **Yes**.

7.  With the App-V Sequencer now installed, launch Windows Defender, navigate to **Settings | Administrator**, and remove the mark from **Turn on this app**.

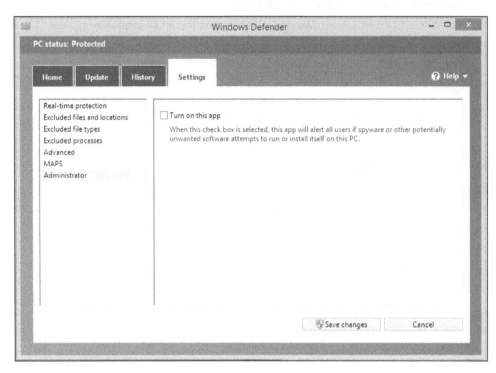

8.  Click on **Save changes** and **Close** on the message that appears regarding Windows Defender no longer protecting your PC.

 Be sure to uninstall any other antivirus/malware programs from your sequencing computers as their presence measurably slows down the capture process and can interfere with the correct capture of the virtual application.

9. Launch `services.msc`, set the **Windows Search** service to **disabled**, and then **stop** the service.

10. Shut down the virtual machine and then create a virtual machine snapshot.

 Creating a snapshot at this stage allows you to quickly go back to a known clean state, allowing you to sequence many virtual applications without setting up a new operating system installation each time.

# Sequencing the Audacity sound editor

Almost all applications can be virtualized with varying degrees of ease. Applications such as Audacity, which do not have a complex licensing framework or require the installation of system services or prerequisite applications, can be sequenced in minutes. This recipe shows you how to create such a package.

## Getting ready

To complete these steps, you will need to have completed all of the steps in the first recipe of this chapter.

## How to do it...

The following list shows you the high-level steps involved in this recipe and the tasks required to complete the recipe (all of the actions in this recipe will take place on the sequencing client called WIN8SEQUENCER):

- ▸ Download the Audacity sound editor installer.
- ▸ Begin the capture process.
- ▸ Install the application.
- ▸ Optimize the application for streaming.
- ▸ End the capture process and generate the App-V application.

 Before capturing an application, it is worth performing a "dry run" of the installation first to see how the installer works and determine any pre or post installation tasks.

The implementation of the preceding tasks is as follows:

1. Start WIN8SEQUENCER.
2. Visit `http://audacityteam.org/` and download the installer version of Audacity, saving it to your downloads folder.
3. Launch the App-V sequencer, accepting any **User Account Control** prompts by clicking **Yes**.
4. Click on **Create a New Virtual Application Package**.

5. With **Create Package (default)** selected, click on **Next**.

6. Review any warnings about the current system state (correcting the issues listed where possible) and click on **Next**.

 Completing steps 6-8 of the previous recipe will have prevented any warnings appearing on a clean Windows 8.1 image. However, depending on the software installed on your base image, there may be other issues to address.

7. With **Standard Application (default)** selected click on **Next**.

8. At the **Select Installer** screen, click on **Browse** and navigate to the Audacity installer you saved in your downloads folder, select the installer, and then click on **Next**.

9. Set **Virtual Application Package Name** to `Audacity 2.0.6` and click on **Next**.

10. Wait for the Audacity installer to launch; do not attempt to launch the installer yourself and do not interact with the App-V sequencer until the installation is finished.

11. With the installer launched and with **English** selected as the installation language, click on **OK**.

12. Click on **Next** to proceed with the installation, review the software license, and click on **Next**.

13. Ensure the installation path is set to a subfolder in the `Program Files` or `Program Files (x86)` folder and click on **Next**.

 In previous versions, you would set a primary virtual application directory, which the App-V sequencer would monitor for changes. This requirement has been removed in App-V 5 SP3 but can be turned back on again by following the instructions at `http://technet.microsoft.com/en-us/library/dn858700.aspx`.

14. Review the additional tasks screen and click on **Next**. Click on the **Install** button to begin the installation.

15. Review any post-installation screens, making sure that you do not have **Launch Audacity** selected at the final stage of the installation.

16. With the installation complete, tick the **I am finished installing** checkbox in the App-V sequencer and click on **Next**.

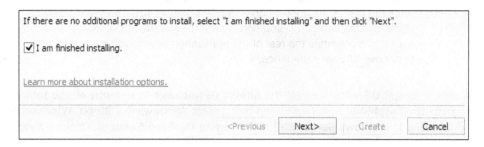

17. The App-V sequencer will now detect any new applications installed on the computer and present you with a list of the detected applications. At this stage, you can launch the applications to complete any first-use tasks (for example, accepting a licensing agreement or configuring application settings). Click on **Next** to proceed.

18. Review the installation report; on completed applications, the App-V sequencer may suggest tasks to complete at this stage to ensure the application runs as expected. Click on **Next** to continue.

19. At the **Customize** screen, select the **Customize** radio button and click on **Next**.

20. At the streaming screen, click on **Run All**. Once Audacity has launched, close any open Audacity windows and return to the App-V sequencer and click on **Next**.

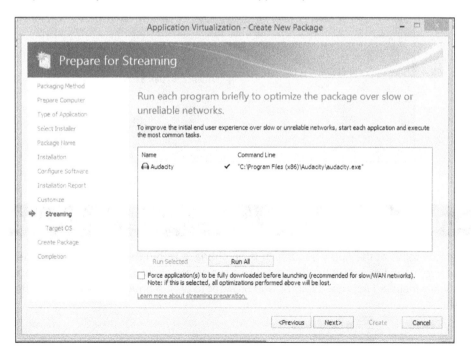

Application streaming detects which components of the applications are required to get the application into a launched state (if not fully functional while the rest of the application is downloaded). Utilizing streaming allows users who might be on a slow connection to have the application in a launched state while the rest of the application downloads, thus creating a better overall user experience.

21. At the **Target OS** screen, select the **Allow this package to run only on the following operating systems** radio button and then select **Windows 8.1 32-bit**, **Windows 8.1 64-bit**, and **Windows Server 2012 R2 Remote Desktop Services**. Click on **Next** to proceed.

22. At the **Create Package** screen, make a note of the default save location for the package and click on **Create**.

23. Review the **Completion** screen and click on **Close** to finish the packaging process.

24. Finally, copy and paste the folder that the App-V sequencer created on your desktop into the `\\demo.org\app-v` folder. Shut down the virtual machine and revert it to the snapshot that you created earlier.

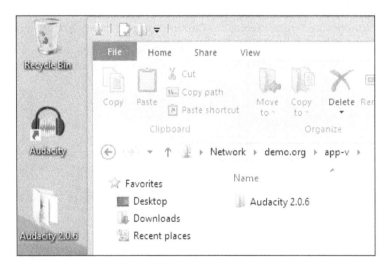

# Sequencing an Internet Explorer shortcut

Although the focus of the App-V sequencer is on changes within the Program Files folders, it is also very useful at capturing shortcuts. This recipe will show you how to use a shortcut to the locally installed Internet Explorer web browser to create an App-V deployed shortcut to a website.

## Getting ready

To complete these steps, you will need to have completed all of the steps in the recipe, *Setting up the sequencer*, of this chapter.

## How to do it...

The following list shows you the high-level steps involved in this recipe and the tasks required to complete the recipe (all of the actions in this recipe will take place on the sequencing client called WIN8SEQUENCER):

- ▸ Begin the capture process.
- ▸ Create the shortcut.
- ▸ End the capture process and generate the App-V application.

The implementation of the preceding tasks is as follows:

1. Start WIN8SEQUENCER.
2. Launch the App-V sequencer accepting any **User Account Control** prompts by clicking on **Yes**.
3. Click on **Create a New Virtual Application Package**.
4. With **Create Package (default)** selected, click on **Next**.
5. Review any warnings about the current system state (correcting the issues listed, where possible) and click on **Next**.
6. With **Standard Application (default)** selected, click on **Next**.
7. Select the **Perform a custom installation** radio button and click on **Next**.
8. Set **Virtual Application Package Name** to `Audacity Website Shortcut` and click on **Next**.
9. Once the sequencer reaches the installation screen, right-click on your Desktop and select **New | Shortcut**.

10. In the window that appears, set `"C:\Program Files (x86)\Internet Explorer\iexplore.exe" http://audacityteam.org` as the location of the item and click on **Next**.

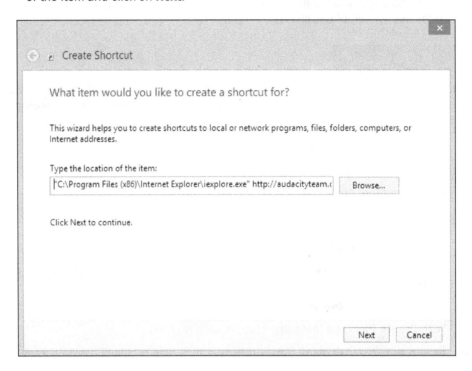

11. Set the name of the shortcut to `Audacity website` and click on **Finish**.

12. Open Windows Explorer and navigate to `C:\ProgramData\Microsoft\Windows\Start Menu\Programs`. Copy and paste the shortcut you just created into the root of the folder, accepting any **User Account Control** prompts by clicking on **Continue**.

13. Back in the App-V sequencer, tick the **I am finish installing** box and click on **Next**.

14. Review the **Configure Software** and **Installation Report** pages, clicking **Next** to continue.

15. At the customization page, accept the default of **Stop now** and click on **Next** to continue.

16. Make a note of the save location for the App-V package, and click on **Create** to complete the sequencing process.

17. Review the **Completion page** and then copy and paste the generated folder here: `\\demo.org\app-v`. Shut down the virtual machine and revert it to the snapshot that you created earlier.

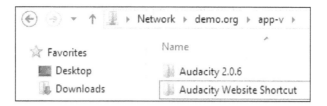

# Sequencing an application hosted on a network share

Occasionally, applications may be hosted on network shares or network drives. Just as with Internet Explorer shortcuts, App-V can be used to deploy a shortcut to this application even though it does not capture files as well.

## Getting ready

To complete these steps, you will need to have completed all of the steps in the recipe, *Setting up the sequencer*, of this chapter.

## How to do it...

The following list shows you the high-level steps involved in this recipe and the tasks required to complete the recipe (all of the actions in this recipe will take place on the sequencing client called WIN8SEQUENCER):

  ▸ Download the Audacity ZIP file and copy the contents to a network share.
  ▸ Begin the capture process.
  ▸ Create the shortcut.
  ▸ End the capture process and generate the App-V application.

Prior to App-V 5 SP2 Hotfix 4, the NTFS permissions on any application hosted on a network share had to be set to allow the Active Directory account of the computer running the App-V client to have permission to access the share. This requirement has since been removed and App-V applications now look to the users' Active Directory permissions instead.

The implementation of the preceding tasks is as follows:

1. Start WIN8SEQUENCER.
2. Navigate to `http://audacityteam.org` and select **Other Audacity Downloads for Windows**.

3. Download the Audacity 2.0.6 ZIP file and extract the contents to `\\demo.org\FileStore\Audacity`.

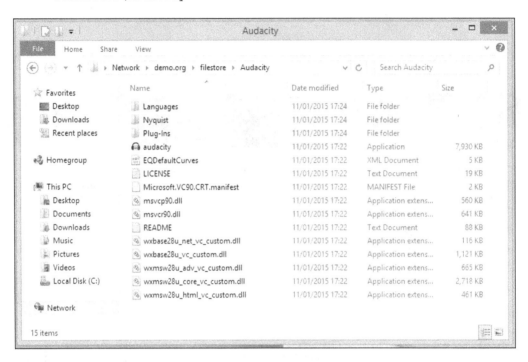

4. Launch the App-V sequencer, accepting any **User Account Control** prompts by clicking on **Yes**.

5. Click on **Create a New Virtual Application Package**.

6. With **Create Package (default)** selected, click on **Next**.

7. Review any warnings about the current system state (correcting the issues listed, where possible) and click on **Next**.

8. With **Standard Application (default)** selected, click on **Next**.

9. Select the **Perform a custom installation** radio button and click on **Next**.

10. Set the **Virtual Application Package Name** to `Audacity Network Share` and click on **Next**.

11. Once the sequencer reaches the installation screen, right-click on your Desktop and select **New | Shortcut**.

12. In the window that appears, set **"\\demo.org\filestore\Audacity\audacity.exe"** as the location of the item and click on **Next**.

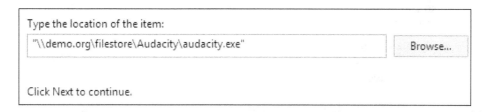

Type the location of the item:

"\\demo.org\filestore\Audacity\audacity.exe"      Browse...

Click Next to continue.

13. Set the name of the shortcut to `Audacity Network Share` and click on **Finish**.

14. Open Windows Explorer, navigate to `C:\ProgramData\Microsoft\Windows\Start Menu\Programs`, and copy and paste the shortcut you just created into the root of the folder, accepting any **User Account Control** prompts by clicking on **Continue**.

15. Back in the App-V sequencer, tick the **I am finished installing** box and click on **Next**.

16. Review the **Configure Software** and **Installation Report** pages, clicking on **Next** to continue.

17. On the **Customize** page, accept the default of **Stop now** and click on **Next** to continue.

18. Make a note of the save location for the App-V package and click on **Create** to complete the sequencing process.

19. Review the **Completion** page and then copy and paste the generated folder here: `\\demo.org\app-v`. Shut down the virtual machine and revert it to the snapshot that you created earlier.

# Dissecting an App-V 5 package

App-V packages can be edited after being captured using the sequencer. This recipe shows what the relevance of each file in the package is and how to edit it.

The following screenshot shows the contents of the package using the Audacity installation captured in the second recipe of this chapter:

The following table explains the purpose of each of these files:

| | |
|---|---|
| `.appv` | The App-V Virtual Application, which contains files, registry entries, and settings. |
| `.msi` | A Microsoft scripted installer, which can be used to deploy the App-V application through Electronic Software Distribution. |
| `_DeploymentConfig.xml` | Package-level publishing options for all applications in the package, including shortcuts, scripting, and file type associations. |
| `_UserConfig.xml` | User-level publishing options for all applications in the package, including shortcuts, scripting, and file type associations. |
| `report.xml` | Lists any output from the capture report, including files that might have been excluded. |

The .xml files can be read/edited using any text editor. However, I prefer Notepad++, which can be downloaded from http://notepad-plus-plus.org.

## Getting ready

To complete these steps, you will need to have completed all of the steps in the first and second recipes of this chapter.

## How to do it...

The following list shows you the high-level steps involved in this recipe and the tasks required to complete the recipe (all of the actions in this recipe will take place on the sequencing client called WIN8SEQUENCER):

- ▸ Load the .appv file in the App-V sequencer.
- ▸ Change the supported operating systems of a package.
- ▸ Modify the file system of a package.
- ▸ Save the modifications as a new package (branching).

The implementation of the preceding tasks is as follows:

1. Start WIN8SEQUENCER.
2. Navigate to \\demo.org\app-v and copy and paste the Audacity 2.0.6 package which you created in the second recipe of this chapter onto your desktop.
3. Open the folder you just copied and pasted and open the Audacity 2.0.6.appv file (which will launch in the App-V sequencer).

 Take note of the size of the .appv file as it changes due to the modifications made in this recipe.

4. Accept any **User Account Control** prompts by clicking on **Yes**.

5. Select **Edit Package** and click on **Next**.

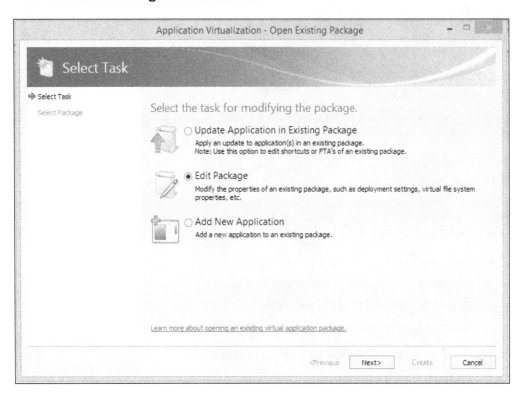

6. Click the **Edit** button to launch the package editor.

7. To view information about the version of the App-V sequencer that was used to make the original package along with the operating system version and processor type, visit the **Change History** tab.

8. To allow the package to run on any version of Windows, select the **Deployment** tab and then move the operating systems listed under **Selected** into **Available**. Note that **(Any Operating System)** now appears under the **Selected** pane.

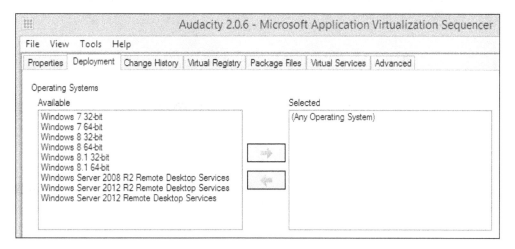

9. To modify the file system of the package, navigate to the **Package Files** tab, expand **Package | Root | VFS | ProgramFilesX86 | Audacity**, right-click on the `help` folder, and press **Delete** to remove it.

10. Accept any prompts that appear as the result of this deletion by clicking **Yes**.

11. To save the changes as an entirely new package, browse to **File | Save As New Package...**.

12. Create a new folder on your desktop called `Audacity 2.0.6 - No help files` and save the new package within that folder.

13. Note that the two packages have significantly different file sizes (caused by the deletion of the help files).

# Scripting in App-V 5

App-V allows the running of scripts and other applications at the time of launch. This can be a particularly useful feature if applications have complex licensing requirements (for example, a license key must be applied each time the application launches) or if the virtual application requires a network drive to be mapped.

## Getting ready

To complete these steps, you will need to have completed all of the steps in the first and second recipes of this chapter.

>  By default, App-V 5 comes with scripting turned off. You can enable it through Group Policy or by running the following PowerShell command on the client:
>
> `Set-AppvClientConfiguration -EnablePackageScripts $true`

## How to do it...

The following list shows you the high-level steps involved in this recipe and the tasks required to complete the recipe (all of the actions in this recipe will take place on the sequencing client called WIN8SEQUENCER):

- ▶ Create a folder named `Resources` within the `FileStore DFS` path.
- ▶ Create a script that will map a network drive and store it within the virtual application.
- ▶ Modify the `_DeploymentConfig.xml` file to run the script.

The implementation of the preceding tasks is as follows:

1. Start WIN8SEQUENCER.
2. Create a new folder called `Resources` in the DFS path `\\demo.org\FileStore`.
3. Open Notepad and enter the following code:

```
Net use Z: \\demo.org\filestore\resources
Set-ExecutionPolicy Restricted
```

4. Save the file as `mapdrive.ps1` on your desktop.
5. Navigate to `\\demo.org\app-v` and copy and paste the `Audacity 2.0.6` package that you created in the second recipe of this chapter onto your desktop.
6. Open the folder you just pasted and open the `Audacity 2.0.6.appv` file (which will launch in the App-V sequencer).
7. Accept any **User Account Control** prompts by clicking **Yes**.
8. Select **Edit Package** and click on **Next**.
9. Click on the **Edit** button to launch the package editor.
10. Browse to the **Package Files** tab and expand **Package | Scripts**.

11. Right-click on the **Scripts** folder and click on **Add**.

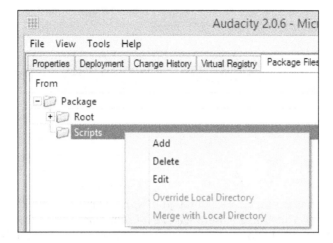

12. Using the **Browse** button in the dialogue window that appears, select the `mapdrive.ps1` file that you created earlier in this recipe, clicking **OK** to add it to the package.

13. Select **File | Save** to save the changes to the package.

14. Open the package `_DeploymentConfig.xml` file and locate the `<UserScripts>` line and remove the comment from above it to enable the scripting features.

```
Remove all of the demo scripts from between the <UserScripts> and
</UserScripts> lines and then enter the
following code-
<StartProcess RunInVirtualEnvironment="false">
  <Path>powershell.exe</Path>
  <Arguments>-ExecutionPolicy RemoteSigned -File
  [{AppVPackageRoot}]\..\Scripts\mapdrive.ps1</Arguments>
  <Wait RollbackOnError="false"/>
  <ApplicationId>[{ProgramFilesX86}]\Audacity\audacity.exe
  </ApplicationId>
</StartProcess>
```

Let's take a look at the following screenshot:

```
234        </Applications>
235        <!-- User Scripts Example - customize and uncomment to use user scripts -->
236
237        <UserScripts>
238            <StartProcess RunInVirtualEnvironment="false">
239                <Path>powershell.exe</Path>
240                <Arguments>-ExecutionPolicy RemoteSigned -File [{AppVPackageRoot}]\..\Scripts\mapdrive.ps1</Arguments>
241                <Wait RollbackOnError="false"/>
242                <ApplicationId>[{ProgramFilesX86}]\Audacity\audacity.exe</ApplicationId>
243            </StartProcess>
244        </UserScripts>
245
246    </UserConfiguration>
```

## How it works...

The command calls powershell.exe (through <Path>, while allowing it to run outside of the virtual environment), instructs PowerShell to set ExectutionPolicy to RemoteSigned (the highest possible setting that allows scripts to run), and then calls the script that maps the network drive.

Note that the path to the mapdrive.ps1 script is the same format as listed in the Package Files tab when examining the .appv package within the sequencer.

# 4
# Managing Packages

In this chapter, we will cover:

- ▸ Publishing a Package to a user group
- ▸ Publishing a Package to a group of machines
- ▸ Managing shortcuts
- ▸ Managing file type associations
- ▸ Testing a package
- ▸ Unpublishing and deleting a package
- ▸ Creating a custom configuration for a security group
- ▸ Deploying an App-V package via MSI

## Introduction

The App-V Management console makes it easy for administrators to publish applications to both groups of machines and users. In addition to this, it can be used to make limited configuration changes to the application.

To complete the recipes in this chapter, you will need to have performed the steps in the first three chapters of this book and have the servers DC, APPV1, APPV2, FS1, FS2, WEB1, and WEB2 running and configured. Additionally, you will need a domain-joined Windows 8.1 computer available to conduct the testing of the virtual application packages.

The applications in this chapter will be deployed with the files hosted on both the SMB shares (FS1 and FS2) and through IIS (WEB1 and WEB2). Ensure that you copy the App-V packages created in *Chapter 3, Sequencing Applications*, to the DFS path at \\demo.org\app-viis in order for them to be used by the web servers.

# Publishing a package to a user group

This recipe shows you how to publish an App-V package to a user group with the application hosted on an SMB share.

## Getting ready

To complete these steps, you will need administrative access to the App-V management console. Also, add the user `Maddy Alans` to the Audacity Users Active Directory Security Group.

## How to do it...

The following list shows you the high-level steps involved in this recipe and the tasks required to complete this recipe (all of the actions in this recipe will take place on a domain-joined Windows 8.1 computer):

▸ Log in to the App-V Management Console.

▸ Add the Audacity package to the console.

▸ Permit the application to be run by the Audacity Users Security Group.

▸ Publish the application.

The implementation of the preceding tasks is as follows:

1. On your Windows 8.1 computer, log in to the App-V Management Console (`http://appv1.demo.org:440/Console.html`) as Sam Adams, the App-V administrator you created in *Chapter 1, Deploying App-V 5 Services.*

2. Click on **ADD or UPGRADE PACKAGES**.

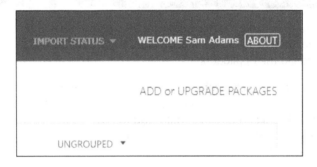

3. In the window that appears, click on **Browse**, navigate to the `\\demo.org\app-v` DFS path, double-click on the `Audacity 2.0.6` folder that you created in *Chapter 3, Sequencing Applications*, and then double-click on the `Audacity 2.0.6.appv` file, as shown here:

ADD or UPGRADE PACKAGES

To import a package specify a UNC or HTTP path. Separate multiple files with semicolons.

`\\demo.org\app-v\Audacity 2.0.6\Audacity 2.0.6.appv`    Browse

Add    Cancel

If you find that instead of displaying the UNC path to the package, you get `C:\fakepath`, you will need to add the address of the App-V Management Console to the list of trusted sites in Internet Explorer.

To do this, navigate to **Settings | Internet Options | Security | Trusted sites | Sites**, untick **Requires server verification**, and set the website address as `http://appv1.demo.org:440/Console.html`.

4. To import the package, click on the **Add** button.

5. A window will then appear confirming that the application has been successfully imported and you will see the package listed in the **Entire Library** pane.

6. To grant the Audacity Users Security Group the permission to access the application, right-click on the package and click on **edit active directory access**.

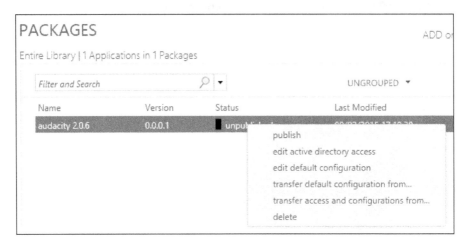

7. In the **FIND VALID ACTIVE DIRECTORY GROUPS AND GRANT ACCESS** box, enter `demo.org\Audacity Users` and then click on the **Check** button.

8. In the drop-down list that appears, select the **Audacity Users** group and then click on **Grant Access** to allow that group access to the package.

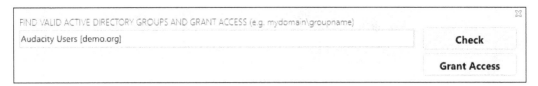

9. Note that the group is now added to the pane below the toolbar and that it uses the default configuration for that package.

10. Finally, to publish the package, right-click on the package and select **Publish**.

 Note that packages can only be assigned to groups and not individual users when using the App-V Management console.

# Publishing a package to a group of machines

This recipe shows you how to publish an App-V package to a machine group with the application hosted on an IIS server.

## Getting ready

To complete these steps, you will need administrative access to the App-V Management Console. In addition, if you haven't done so already, add the user Maddy Alans to the Audacity Users Active Directory Security Group.

## How to do it...

The following list shows you the high-level steps involved in this recipe and the tasks required to complete the recipe (all of the actions in this recipe will take place on a domain-joined Windows 8.1 computer):

- ▶ Log in to the App-V Management Console.
- ▶ Add the Audacity Package to the console.
- ▶ Permit the application to be run by the Domain Computers Security Group.
- ▶ Publish the application.

The implementation of the preceding tasks is as follows:

1. On your Windows 8.1 computer, log in to the App-V Management Console (`http://appv1.demo.org:440/Console.html`) as Sam Adams.

2. Click on **ADD or UPGRADE PACKAGES**.

3. In the window that appears, enter `http://appv.demo.org/Audacity Network Share/Audacity Network Share.appv` (which is the path to the App-V package on the IIS server) and click on **Add**.

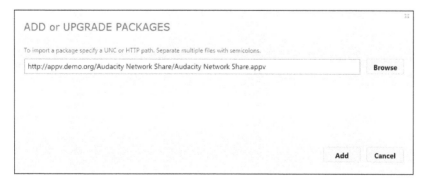

Enabling directory browsing on the web server and opening the root (for example, `http://appv.demo.org`) in a web browser can significantly help in identifying the correct path to use the App-V package.

4. A window will then appear confirming that the application has been successfully imported and you will see the package listed in the **Entire Library** pane.

5. To grant the Domain Computers security group the permission to access the application, right-click on the package and click on **edit active directory access**.

6. In the **FIND VALID ACTIVE DIRECTORY GROUPS AND GRANT ACCESS** box, enter `demo.org\Domain Computers` and then click on the **Check** button.

7. In the drop-down list that appears, select the **Domain Computers** group and then click on **Grant Access** to allow that group access to the package.

8. Note that the group is now added to the pane below the toolbar and that it uses the default configuration for that package.

9. Finally, to publish the package, right-click on the package and select **publish**.

Note that packages can only be assigned to groups and not individual machines when using the App-V Management console.

## How it works...

When adding packages to the Management Console, new rows are added to the App-V SQL database. Using the SQL Server Management Studio, you can examine the tables to view the added rows.

Of particular interest are the Package Versions and Package Entitlements tables, which show the App-V packages and their group assignments, respectively. The following screenshot shows the Package Versions table. Note that **PackageGUID**, **Name**, **VersionGUID**, and **PackageUrl** are all referenced in the table. In addition, a unique ID is provided for each row, which is in turn used with other tables.

| | Id | PackageGuid | Name | VersionGuid | PackageUrl |
|---|---|---|---|---|---|
| 1 | 3025 | B2EFECA5-4BA1-4DD4-B89... | Audacity 2.0.6 | 9144EEE7-ACF3-4ABA-AD67-1... | \\demo.org\app-v\Audacity 2.0.6\Audacity 2.0.6.appv |
| 2 | 3026 | F2464984-3F43-49F0-97BA-... | Audacity Network Share | 797E1888-FC65-45B0-993F-42... | http://appv.demo.org/Audacity Network Share/Audacity Network Share.appv |

Examining the PackageEntitlements table shows the link between the **PackageVersionId** (as seen in the previous table) and **Sid** columns, which corresponds to an Active Directory security group's Security Identifier.

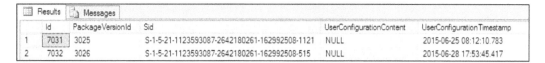

| | Id | PackageVersionId | Sid | UserConfigurationContent | UserConfigurationTimestamp |
|---|---|---|---|---|---|
| 1 | 7031 | 3025 | S-1-5-21-1123593087-2642180261-162992508-1121 | NULL | 2015-06-25 08:12:10.783 |
| 2 | 7032 | 3026 | S-1-5-21-1123593087-2642180261-162992508-515 | NULL | 2015-06-28 17:53:45.417 |

# Managing shortcuts

On occasion, the administrator may wish to add or remove shortcuts to applications within a package; for example, the default Audacity installer generates shortcuts on both the desktop and the Start menu even though only one shortcut is required by the end user. Through the App-V Management Console, these extra shortcuts can be deleted or additional ones can be created.

## Getting ready

To complete these steps, you will need to have completed the first two recipes in this chapter.

## How to do it...

The following list shows you the high-level steps involved in this recipe and the tasks required to complete this recipe (all of the actions in this recipe will take place on a domain-joined Windows 8.1 computer):

- ▸ Log in to the App-V Management Console.
- ▸ Delete the Audacity desktop shortcut.
- ▸ Add an additional shortcut to the Audacity application in the Start menu.

The implementation of the preceding tasks is as follows:

1. On your Windows 8.1 computer, log in to the App-V Management Console (http://appv1.demo.org:440/Console.html) as Sam Adams.
2. Right-click on the **audacity 2.0.6** package and click on **edit default configuration**.
3. In the **Default Configuration** pane that appears, click on **SHORTCUTS**.

4. Right-click on the listed shortcut under **Common Desktop** and click on
   **Remove Shortcut**.

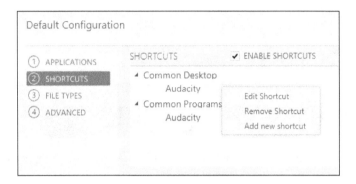

5. To add a new shortcut, click on **Add new shortcut**.

6. In the window that appears, select **Audacity** from the drop-down list under **SELECT THE APPLICATION OR OTHER TARGET FOR THIS SHORTCUT**. From the drop-down list under **Select a standard location as a starting point**, select **START MENU**.

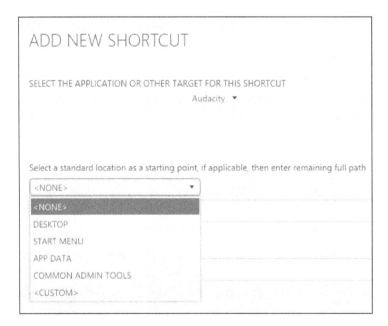

 Setting the standard location as **START MENU** will create shortcuts on the **Start** menu, alternatively, you can select **DESKTOP** to create shortcuts on the user's desktop instead.

7. You will notice that **[{Common Start Menu}]**\ is automatically inserted as the shortcut path for the application. To complete the path, type `Media Tools\` (ensuring that you include the \ symbol). Finally, click on **Add**.

Select a standard location as a starting point, if applicable, then enter remaining full path

START MENU ▾

[{Common Start Menu}]\Media Tools\

PARAMETERS (Optional)

 Note that you can also add command line parameters to the shortcut to use when launching the application.

# Managing file type associations

One of the key advantages of App-V is that it allows you to run multiple and often incompatible editions of the same software (for example, Office 2007 and 2013) side by side; however, this can still cause conflicts with file type associations. Although it is not yet possible to manage file type associations through the App-V management console, it is possible to modify the associations by creating custom files. This recipe shows how to delete any unneeded file type associations.

## Getting ready

To complete these steps, you will need to complete the first recipe in this chapter ensuring that the Audacity Users security group has permission to run Audacity 2.0.6.

## How to do it...

The following list shows you the high-level steps involved in this recipe and the tasks required to complete the recipe (all of the actions in this recipe will take place on a domain-joined Windows 8.1 computer):

▸ Generate a new App-V configuration file.

▸ Edit the configuration file to remove the file type association.

▸ Import and overwrite the stored configuration.

The implementation of the preceding tasks is as follows:

1. On your Windows 8.1 computer, log in to the App-V Management Console (`http://appv1.demo.org:440/Console.html`) as Sam Adams.

2. Right-click on the **audacity 2.0.6** package and select **edit default configuration**.

3. In the **Default Configuration** pane that appears, scroll down and click on **Export Configuration**.

4. In the window that appears, save the new configuration file with the original App-V source files with the filename `Audacity 2.0.6 no file types.xml`.

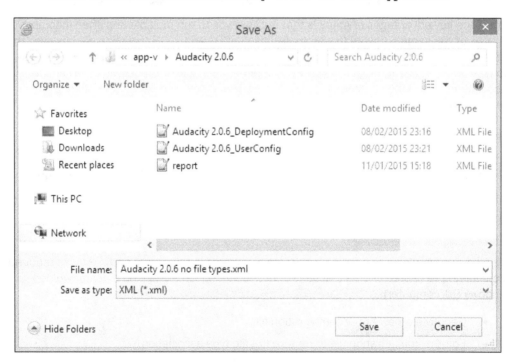

5. Open the source file in your favorite XML editor, identify the AUP to be deleted between the `<Extension Category="AppV.FileTypeAssociation">` `</Extension>` tag (as highlighted in the following screenshot), and either comment or delete the lines to remove the shortcut.

```
\\demo.org\app-v\Audacity 2.0.6\Audacity 2.0.6 no file types.xml - Not
File  Edit  Search  View  Encoding  Language  Settings  Macro  Run  Plugins  Window  ?

 Audacity 2.0.6 no file types.xml

 1   <DeploymentConfiguration xmlns:xsd="http://www.w3.org/2001/XMLSchema" xmlns:xsi="http://www.w3.org
 2     <MachineConfiguration />
 3     <UserConfiguration>
 4       <Subsystems>
 5         <FileTypeAssociations>
 6           <Extensions>
 7             <Extension Category="AppV.FileTypeAssociation">
 8               <FileTypeAssociation>
 9                 <FileExtension>
10                   <Name>.AUP</Name>
11                   <ProgId>Audacity.Project</ProgId>
12                   <ShellNew />
13                 </FileExtension>
14                 <ProgId>
15                   <Name>Audacity.Project</Name>
16                   <Description>Audacity Project File</Description>
17                   <ShellCommands>
18                     <DefaultCommand />
19                     <ShellCommand>
20                       <ApplicationId>[{ProgramFilesX86}]\Audacity\audacity.exe</ApplicationId>
21                       <Name>open</Name>
22                       <CommandLine>"[{ProgramFilesX86}]\Audacity\audacity.exe" "%1"</CommandLine>
23                       <DdeExec />
24                     </ShellCommand>
25                   </ShellCommands>
26                 </ProgId>
27               </FileTypeAssociation>
28             </Extension>
29           </Extensions>
30         </FileTypeAssociations>
```

6. Save the changes to the file and return to the App-V management console.

7. With the Audacity 2.0.6 package still selected, click on **Import and Overwrite this Configuration**. In the window that appears, select the configuration file that you edited and click on **Open**.

8. The App-V Management console will then prompt you to confirm the overwrite, click on the **Overwrite** button to apply the configuration file.

9. With the default configuration pane still open, click on **FILE TYPES** from the left-hand side to confirm that there are no file type associations listed.

# Testing a package

Virtual applications should be thoroughly tested before being deployed to end users; this recipe will show a simple testing methodology for a package.

## Getting ready

To complete these steps you will need to have completed all of the steps in the first, second and third recipes of this chapter.

## How to do it...

The following list shows you the high-level steps involved in this recipe and the tasks required to complete the recipe (all of the actions in this recipe will take place on a domain-joined Windows 8.1 computer):

▸ Confirm that the App-V Publishing server is updated with the latest set of applications.

▸ Log in as Maddy Alans on your testing client.

▸ Confirm that the application appears as intended in the Start menu.

▸ Confirm that the file type associations work as intended.

 When testing a virtual application, you should also check whether the application works as intended with any locally installed applications (for example, a classroom resources application might launch a PowerPoint document or load a file in Windows Media Player).

The implementation of the preceding tasks is as follows:

1. On your Windows 8.1 computer, log in to the App-V Management Console (`http://appv1.demo.org:440/Console.html`) as Sam Adams.

2. On the left-hand side of the console, select **Servers**. You will see a list of all of the App-V Publishing servers in your environment along with the time that they last synced with the Management server to obtain the latest list of application/user assignments.

> The App-V Publishing server will sync periodically with the Management server as part of its normal operation (the default time is 10 minutes), you can force an update by restarting the AppvPublishing application pool on your App-V Publishing server. In addition, you can modify the default sync schedule by setting the registry key `HKEY_LOCAL_MACHINE\SOFTWARE\Microsoft\AppV\Server\PublishingService\ PUBLISHING_MGT_SERVER_REFRESH_INTERVAL` to a smaller value (the default is 600 units which equates to 600 seconds).
>
> Be careful when altering this value; setting it too low will cause unnecessary resource utilization (which can be better used when serving client requests) and setting it too high will cause an unnecessarily long wait for new applications or updates to be published to clients.

3. On your Windows 8.1 computer, log in as `Maddy Alans`.

4. Upon login, the App-V client will automatically reach out to the Publishing server and update the list of applications on the client.

5. Visit the Start menu and note that, after a short pause, the published applications will appear.

6. Create a new Audacity project file and save it to the desktop. Note that the correct icon is displayed on the saved file, and when you run it, the `Audacity` package loads.

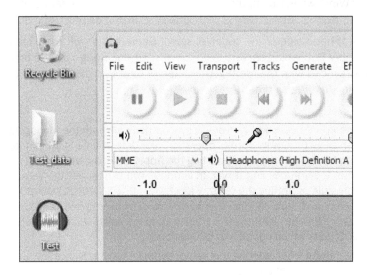

While a user is logged in, depending on your Group Policy settings, the App-V client will periodically reach out to the Publishing server to obtain the latest list of applications. Without logging the user out, you can also force an update by running the following PowerShell command:

```
Get-AppvPublishingServer | Sync-AppvPublishingServer
```

Let's take a look at the following screenshot:

```
Windows PowerShell
Windows PowerShell
Copyright (C) 2013 Microsoft Corporation. All rights reserved.

PS C:\Users\maddy> Get-AppvPublishingServer | Sync-AppvPublishingServer

Id                        : 1
SetByGroupPolicy          : True
Name                      : app-vpublishing
URL                       : http://app-vpublishing.demo.org:441
GlobalRefreshEnabled      : True
GlobalRefreshOnLogon      : True
GlobalRefreshInterval     : 2
GlobalRefreshIntervalUnit : Hour
UserRefreshEnabled        : True
UserRefreshOnLogon        : True
UserRefreshInterval       : 2
UserRefreshIntervalUnit   : Hour
```

# Unpublishing and deleting a package

As part of the normal application deployment life cycle, administrators may unpublish an App-V package, and in doing so, remove it from use from all users. Deleting a package removes all references to it from the management database while leaving the source files intact.

## Getting ready

To complete these steps, you will need to complete all of the steps in the first recipe of this chapter.

## How to do it...

The following list shows you the high-level steps involved in this recipe and the tasks required to complete this recipe (all of the actions in this recipe will take place on a domain-joined Windows 8.1 computer):

-   Log in to the App-V Management Console.
-   Unpublish the package.
-   Verify that the package has been unpublished by testing.

The implementation of the preceding tasks is as follows:

1.  On your Windows 8.1 computer, log in to the App-V Management Console (`http://appv1.demo.org:440/Console.html`) as Sam Adams.

2.  Right-click on the **audacity 2.0.6** package, and from the drop-down menu that appears, click on **unpublish**.

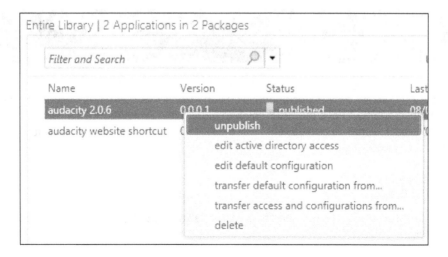

3. Note that the application's status turns to unpublished, and as such, it will no longer be available to users.

4. To delete the package entirely, right-click on it again and select **delete**. An orange confirmation bar will appear at the top of the screen; click on **Confirm** to complete the deletion.

Microsoft
## Application Virtualization

⚠ Are you sure you want to delete the following packages?    <u>Confirm</u>  or  [Cancel]
Audacity 2.0.6

5. You will then receive confirmation of the deletion, click on the cross at the right-hand side of the page to close this confirmation box.

6. On your Windows 8.1 computer, log in as Maddy Alans and allow the App-V client to refresh. Note that the Audacity shortcuts disappear from the Start menu.

## There's more...

If an application has been previously streamed onto the client, the files used to run that application will still be present in the App-V cache (`C:\ProgramData\App-V`). One way to remove these files is to run the elevated PowerShell command `Remove-AppvClientPackage *`.

Note that this will remove all of the packages in the cache even if they are still valid applications.

# Creating a custom configuration for a security group

In addition to modifying the default configuration for an App-V package (for example, to remove superfluous file type associations), you can also create custom configuration files for each security group that have the permission to launch the application. This recipe will show you how to create a custom configuration for the Audacity users group that will automatically launch Audacity upon login.

## Getting ready

To complete these steps, you will need to complete all of the steps in the first recipe of this chapter.

## How to do it...

The following list shows you the high-level steps involved in this recipe and the tasks required to complete the recipe (all of the actions in this recipe will take place on a domain-joined Windows 8.1 computer):

- ► Log in to the App-V Management Console.
- ► Create a custom configuration for the Audacity Users security group.
- ► Create a custom shortcut to Audacity in the users start-up folder.

The implementation of the preceding tasks is as follows:

1.  On your Windows 8.1 computer, log in to the App-V Management Console (`http://appv1.demo.org:440/Console.html`) as Sam Adams.

2.  Right-click on the **audacity 2.0.6** package and select **edit active directory access**.

3.  In the bottom pane, set the **ASSIGNED CONFIGURATION** option for **Demo\Audacity Users** to **Custom**, and then click on the **EDIT** link that appears.

4.  In the bottom pane, select **shortcuts** and click on **Add new shortcut**.

5.  In the window that appears, set the Application target as **Audacity**, the location of the shortcut as `[{Startup}]\`, and then click on **Add**.

# Deploying an App-V package via MSI

Through using Electronic Software Distribution in addition to deploying packages through the App-V Management console, it is possible to use Microsoft Group Policy Objects to deploy the **Microsoft Scripted Installer** (**MSI**) for a package, which is automatically generated by the sequencer.

A key advantage of this deployment method is that you do not need to maintain an App-V Management server or Publishing server.

This recipe will show you how to use this method to deploy App-V Packages.

[  Note that you still need the App-V client installed on the machine that you wish to target with this method of deployment. ]

## Getting ready

To complete the steps in this recipe, you need to create the Audacity website's shortcut App-V package explained in *Chapter 3, Sequencing Applications*.

## How to do it...

The following list shows you the high-level steps involved in this recipe and the tasks required to complete this recipe (all of the actions in this recipe will take place on the server DC):

- ▶ Create a new Group Policy Object.
- ▶ Deploy the Audacity website's shortcut package using managed software installation.

The implementation of the preceding tasks is as follows:

1. On the server DC, launch the Group Policy management console.
2. Expand the tree structure to show the **Domain Computers Organizational Unit** option. Right-click on it and select **Create a GPO in this domain, and Link it here...**
3. Set the name of the policy as App-V Deploy Audacity Website Shortcut, and click on **OK**.
4. Right-click on the newly created policy, and click on **Edit....**
5. In the window that appears, right-click on the policy and click on **Properties**.
6. Tick **Disable User Configuration settings** and click on **OK** (accepting any warning prompts) to return to the Group Policy Management Editor.
7. Navigate to **Computer Configuration** | **Policies** | **Software Settings**.

8.  Right-click on **Software installation** and navigate to **New | Package....**

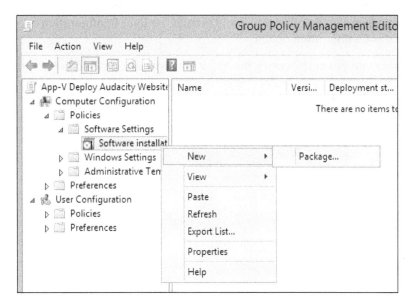

9.  In the window that appears, navigate to the `\\demo.org\app-v\Audacity Website Shortcut` path and double-click on the `Audacity Website Shortcut.msi` file shown.

10. In the next window that appears, select the **Assigned** option and click on **OK**.

11. The application will now appear in the Editor and will be installed on the targeted computer during its next reboot.

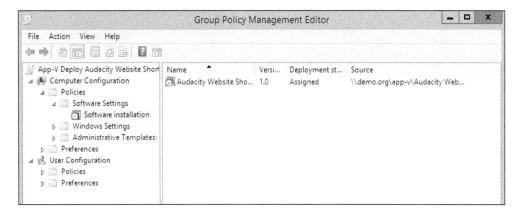

You can also use this method of deployment with users instead of groups. When creating the Group Policy object, simply set it to target an OU containing users. Ensure that you disable the computer settings in step 6 and in step 7 and expand the **User Configuration** option instead of the **Computer Configuration** option.

In addition, although you are not using the App-V Management server or a Publishing server in this configuration, you can still deploy a Reporting server to gather insights on the users who are using the App-V applications.

# 5
# Using Connection Groups

In this chapter, we will cover:

- ▶ Sequencing the Java Development Kit
- ▶ Sequencing Greenfoot
- ▶ Connecting the applications via a connection group
- ▶ Testing the application

## Introduction

The connection groups feature allows for multiple virtualized applications to communicate with each other. Typically, this feature is used when an administrator wishes to virtualize middleware applications (for example, the Java Development Kit) or a plugin (for example, a Microsoft Office add-in) to be used with other App-V packages.

It's worth noting that Connection Groups (previously known as Dynamic Suite Composition in App-V 4) received a major overhaul in App-V 5 SP3, and as such, please ensure that you are running at least version number 5.0.10107 on the sequencer, client, and server.

Finally, as of App-V 5, SP2 Microsoft provides full support for virtualizing the Microsoft C++ runtimes as a middleware package.

# Sequencing the Java Development Kit

The Java Development Kit will serve as our middleware package and is a prerequisite for the Greenfoot development software. Note that middleware differs from plugins, in that, middleware is typically required to make another program run while a plugin is used to enhance the abilities of another application (for example, Adobe Flash would be a plugin for Internet Explorer).

## Getting ready

To complete these steps, you will need to have completed the first recipe of *Chapter 3, Sequencing Applications*, where you created a virtual machine to capture App-V packages.

## How to do it...

The following list shows you the high-level steps involved in this recipe and the tasks required to complete the recipe (all of the actions in this recipe will take place on the sequencing client called WIN8SEQUENCER):

▶  Download the Java Development Kit.

▶  Begin the capture process.

▶  Install the Java Development Kit.

▶  Finish the capture process and upload to the App-V server.

The implementation of the preceding tasks is as follows:

1.  Start WIN8SEQUENCER.

2.  Visit `http://www.oracle.com/technetwork/java/javase/downloads/` and download the latest version of **Java Development Kit** (**JDK**) for Windows x64, and save it to your desktop.

3.  Launch the App-V sequencer, accepting any **User Account Control** prompts by clicking on **Yes**.

4.  Click on **Create a New Virtual Application Package**.

5.  With **Create Package (default)** selected, click on **Next**.

6.  Review any warnings about the current system state (correcting the issues listed where possible) and click on **Next**.

7.  On the **Type of Application** screen, select **Middleware** and then click on **Next**.

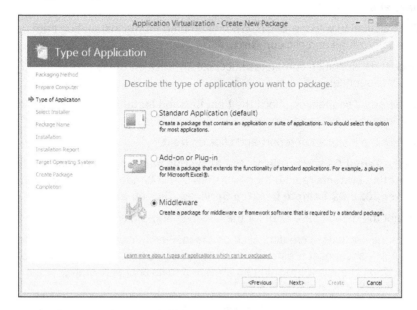

8.  Set the JDK executable that you downloaded in step 2 as the installer and then click on **Next**.

9.  Set the **Virtual Application Package Name** option as JDK <version number> (in this example, I will use JDK 8u31) and click on **Next**.

10. Allow the JDK installer to start and click on **Next** to begin the installation process.

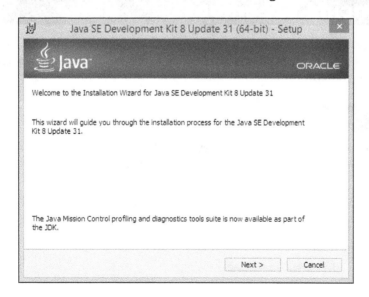

11. On the **Optional Features** screen, set all the options to be installed on the local hard drive and click on **Next**.

12. The installation will now begin. When prompted for the installation path, accept the default provided and click on **Next**.

13. Once the installation completes successfully, click on **Close** and return to the App-V sequencer.

14. In the App-V sequencer, check the **I am finished installing** box and click on **Next** to continue the packaging process.

15. Review the installation report and click on **Next**.

16. On the **Target OS** screen, select the **Allow this package to run only on the following operating systems** radio button and then select **Windows 8.1 64-bit** and **Windows Server 2012 R2 Remote Desktop Services**. Click on **Next** to proceed.

17. Accept the default save path for the package and click on **Create**.

18. Once the package is created, click on **Close**. Finally, copy and paste the folder that the App-V sequencer created on your desktop into the \\demo.org\app-v folder. Shut down the virtual machine and return it to its snapshot state.

 If you are sequencing Java as a plugin instead of sequencing it as middleware, do not attempt to launch any element of Java during the sequencing process. Doing so can create temporary files, which the App-V sequencer will not detect and can cause problems later on when attempting to launch the plugin on another computer.

# Sequencing Greenfoot

**Greenfoot** is a development package aimed at teaching object orientation to children. It is based on Java and is largely platform independent. In this recipe, you will package Greenfoot without including the JDK.

## Getting ready

To complete these steps, you will need to have completed the first recipe of *Chapter 3*, *Sequencing Applications*, where you created a virtual machine to capture App-V packages.

## How to do it...

The following list shows you the high-level steps involved in this recipe and the tasks required to complete the recipe (all of the actions in this recipe will take place on the sequencing client called WIN8SEQUENCER):

- ▸ Download Greenfoot.
- ▸ Begin the capture process.
- ▸ Install Greenfoot.
- ▸ Finish the capture process and upload it to the App-V server.

The implementation of the preceding tasks is as follows:

1. Start WIN8SEQUENCER.
2. Visit `http://www.greenfoot.org/download`, and, under other versions, download the Windows version without the bundled JDK version and save it to your desktop.
3. Launch the App-V sequencer, accepting any **User Account Control** prompts by clicking on **Yes**.
4. Click on **Create a New Virtual Application Package**.
5. With **Create Package (default)** selected, click on **Next**.
6. Review any warnings about the current system state (correcting the issues listed where possible) and click on **Next**.
7. On the **Type of Application** screen, select **Standard Application** and then click on **Next**.
8. Set the installer for the application as the Greenfoot executable you downloaded in step 2 and click on **Next**.
9. Set the **Virtual Application Package Name** option as `Greenfoot <version number>` (in this example, I will use Greenfoot 2.4.1) and click on **Next**.

10. Once the Greenfoot installer launches, click on **Next** to begin the installation process.

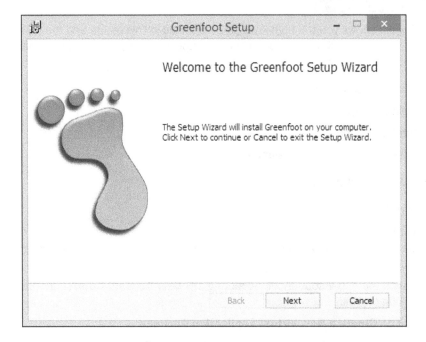

11. Set the installation scope to **Install for all users of this machine** and click on **Next**.

12. Accept the default file associations and shortcuts and click on **Next**.

13. Accept the default installation path and click on **Next**.

14. Click on **Install** to begin the installation of Greenfoot.

15. Once the installation is complete, click on **Finish** and return to the App-V sequencer.

16. In the App-V sequencer, check the **I am finished installing** box and click on **Next** to continue the packaging process.

17. On the **Configure Software** screen, do not run any of the applications and click on **Next**.

18. Review the installation report and click on **Next**.

19. On the **Customize** screen, select the **Customize** radio option and click on **Next**.

20. On the **Streaming** screen, do not run any of the applications and click on **Next**, accepting any dialogue windows that appear.

21. On the **Target OS** screen, select the **Allow this package to run only on the following operating systems** radio button and then select **Windows 8.1 64-bit** and **Windows Server 2012 R2 Remote Desktop Services**. Click on **Next** to proceed.

22. Accept the default save path for the package and click on **Create**.

23. Once the package is created, click on **Close**. Finally, copy and paste the folder that the App-V sequencer created on your desktop into the `\\demo.org\app-v` folder. Shut down the virtual machine and return it to its snapshot state.

# Connecting the applications via a connection group

With both the JDK and Greenfoot packages created, we can now add them to the App-V management console and create a connection group. This recipe will show you how to create the connection group.

## Getting ready

To complete these steps, you will need administrative access to the App-V management console. Add the user `Maddy Alans` to the Greenfoot users active directory security group. In addition to this, using the recipes in *Chapter 4*, *Managing Packages*, publish both the JDK and Greenfoot packages to the Greenfoot Users Active Directory Security Group.

Let's take a look at the following screenshot:

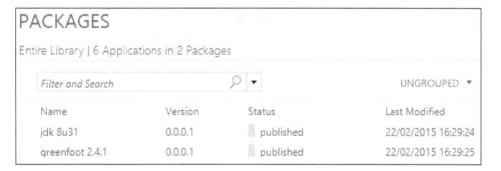

## How to do it...

The following list shows you the high-level steps involved in this recipe and the tasks required to complete the recipe (all of the actions in this recipe will take place on a domain-joined Windows 8.1 computer):

▸ Log in as `Sam Adams` and create the App-V connection group.

The implementation of the preceding task is as follows:

1. On your Windows 8.1 computer, log in to the App-V Management Console (`http://appv1.demo.org:440/Console.html`) as `Sam Adams`.

2. Click on **PACKAGES**. From the sidebar that appears, click on **CONNECTION GROUPS**.

3. In the top-right corner of the screen, click on **ADD CONNECTION GROUP**.

4. Set the name of the connection group by clicking on the group name (newly created groups will be called **New Connection Group**) and changing it to `Greenfoot and JDK`.

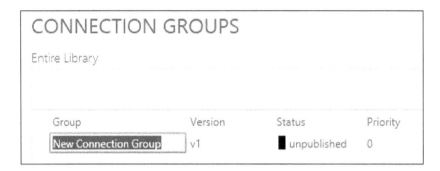

5. Next to **CONNECTED PACKAGES**, click on **EDIT**.

6. In the bottom pane on the screen, add **JDK 8u31** and **Greenfoot 2.4.1** to the connection group by selecting the package from the **PACKAGES Entire Library** option's side and using the left arrow to move it to the connection group. Click on **Apply** and then click on **Close** once done:

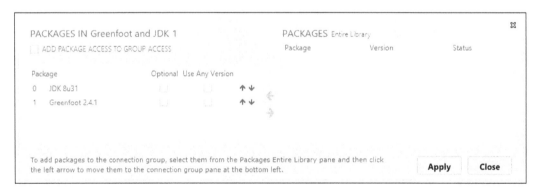

Note that the JDK is at position 0 while Greenfoot is at position 1—this order of precedence decides the order in which the files are loaded within the 'App-V bubble'. Applications with a lower number in the order will have precedence over the others.

As the application (in this case Greenfoot) will not be launched until all of the files in all of the applications have loaded, the position of Greenfoot or the JDK at 0 does not matter in this case.

7. Next to the **ADD ACCESS** option, click on **EDIT**.

8. In the **FIND VALID ACTIVE DIRECTORY GROUPS AND GRANT ACCESS** box, enter `demo.org\Greenfoot Users`, and then click on the **Check** button.

9. In the drop-down list that appears, select the **Greenfoot Users** group and then click on **Grant Access** to allow that group to access the package.

10. Finally, right-click on the connection group and click on **publish** from the drop-down menu that appears.

## There's more...

As part of the improvements made in App-V 5 SP3, when selecting the packages to be used by the connection group, it is possible to set packages as **Optional**; an optional package might be one that is not available to all users due to a licensing number restriction or other circumstance.

If the package is not set as optional (while marked as unpublished or if the user is not permitted to use that application) and the user attempts to run a program in the connection group, App-V will generate an error message and will not load.

# Testing the application

If you were to launch Greenfoot without the connection group in place, you would get an error message similar to the following one. However, with the connection group active, Greenfoot will be able to access the files stored within the JDK package and launch successfully.

## Getting ready

To complete these steps, you will need to have completed all of the other recipes in this chapter.

## How to do it...

The following list shows you the high-level steps involved in this recipe and the tasks required to complete the recipe (all of the actions in this recipe will take place on a domain-joined Windows 8.1 computer):

- ▶ Confirm that the App-V Publishing server is updated with the latest set of applications.
- ▶ Log in as `Maddy Alans` on your testing client.
- ▶ Confirm that the application appears as intended in the **Start** menu and on the desktop.
- ▶ Confirm that the connection group is working as expected.

The implementation of the preceding tasks is as follows:

1. On your Windows 8.1 computer, log in to the App-V Management Console (`http://appv1.demo.org:440/Console.html`) as `Sam Adams`.

2. On the left-hand side of the console, select **servers**. You will see a list of all of the App-V Publishing servers in your environment along with the time that they last synced with the Management server to obtain the latest list of application/user assignments. Assuming that this is the time since you created the connection group, continue to the next step; if not, refresh the page until the Publishing server updates.

3. On your Windows 8.1 computer, log in as `Maddy Alans`.

4. Allow the App-V client to update the assignments for the user and attempt to launch Greenfoot. With the connection group in place, it will launch normally.

5. To confirm that the Connection Group is running, launch a PowerShell (while Greenfoot is still loaded) session and run `Get-AppvConnectionGroup`. The output will list the connection groups assigned to that machine and also indicate which connection groups are active.

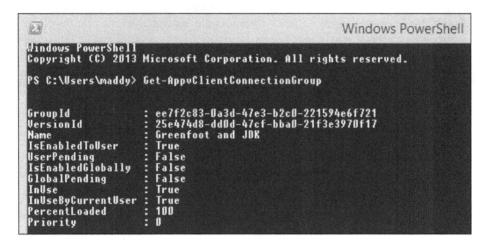

```
                                                          Windows PowerShell
Windows PowerShell
Copyright (C) 2013 Microsoft Corporation. All rights reserved.

PS C:\Users\maddy> Get-AppvClientConnectionGroup

GroupId              : ee7f2c83-0a3d-47e3-b2c0-221594e6f721
VersionId            : 25e474d8-dd0d-47cf-bba0-21f3e3970f17
Name                 : Greenfoot and JDK
IsEnabledToUser      : True
UserPending          : False
IsEnabledGlobally    : False
GlobalPending        : False
InUse                : True
InUseByCurrentUser   : True
PercentLoaded        : 100
Priority             : 0
```

# 6
# Sequencing Office 2013

In this chapter, we will cover:

- Obtaining the Office 2013 App-V package
- Enabling scripting and publishing in Office 2013
- Customizing the Office 2013 App-V package
- Sequencing an Office 2013 plugin

## Introduction

Courtesy of the new **Office Deployment Tool** (**ODT**), sequencing may not be the correct term when referring to App-V 5 and Office 2013. ODT downloads (according to your customizations) the latest Microsoft-generated package for Office 2013 and includes updates with any new features. In addition, it is possible to run ODT as part of a scheduled task. This continuously updates the App-V package, thus saving the administrator a significant amount of time.

| Office version | Sequencing | OS integrations (Windows search, Shell extensions, and so on) | Extra steps required to make it work |
| --- | --- | --- | --- |
| Office 2007 | Recipes available | None | A patch is required to make software licensing work |
| Office 2010 | Package accelerators available | Optional (a patch is required to enable) | A patch is required to make software licensing work |
| Office 2013 + App-V 5 pre SP2 | Package accelerators available | Full | None |

| Office version | Sequencing | OS integrations (Windows search, Shell extensions, and so on) | Extra steps required to make it work |
|---|---|---|---|
| Office 2013 + App-V 5 post SP2 | Not required— download the package from Microsoft | Full | None |

Please note that the method used in this guide applies to App-V 5 SP2 and higher.

# Obtaining the Office 2013 App-V package

In this recipe, we will cover the steps to download the Office 2013 App-V package from the Microsoft repository using ODT.

## Getting ready

To complete these steps, you will need to complete the recipes in *Chapter 1, Deploying App-V 5 Services*, and have the **Notepad++** tool (which can be downloaded for free from `http://notepad-plus-plus.org`) installed on the server APPV1.

## How to do it...

The following list shows you the high-level steps involved in this recipe and the tasks required to complete this recipe (all of the actions in this recipe will take place on the server `APPV1`):

   ▶   Download and install ODT.

   ▶   Create a basic `configuration.xml` file.

   ▶   Download the Office 2013 source files.

   ▶   Generate the App-V package.

The implementation of the preceding tasks is as follows:

   1.   On the server APPV1, visit `https://www.microsoft.com/en-us/download/details.aspx?id=36778` and download the Office Deployment Tool for click-to-run and save it to `C:\Temp`.

2. Once downloaded, browse to `C:\Temp` and run `officedeploymenttool.exe`, accept any licensing prompts and set the folder to save the extracted files to `C:\ODT`. Once the files have been extracted, you can delete the `C:\Temp` folder.

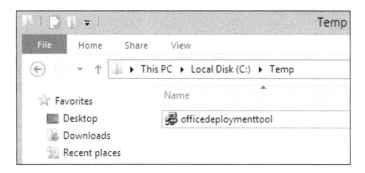

3. Browse to `C:\ODT`, right-click on the `configuration.xml` file, and select **Edit with Notepad++**.

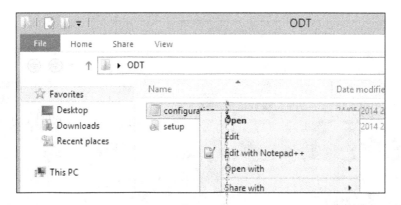

4. Delete the default contents of the file and replace them with the following code snippet:

```
<Configuration>
  <Add SourcePath="\\demo.org\filestore\Office 2013 Source"
  OfficeClientEdition="32" >
    <Product ID="ProPlusVolume">
      <Language ID="en-us" />
    </Product>
  </Add>
</Configuration>
```

5. This XML will instruct the downloader to download the 32-bit edition of Office 2013 Professional Plus Volume Licence Edition with the English United States Language Pack and save the source files to `\\demo.org\filestore\Office 2013 Source`. Save the changes and exit Notepad++.

6. Launch an administrative command prompt and run the following commands to change the directory to `C:\ODT`, and then begin the download process:

```
cd C:\ODT
setup.exe /download .\configuration.xml
```

7. Once the download is complete, examine the file size of the `\\demo.org\filestore\Office 2013 Source` folder. With the default `configuration.xml` used earlier, it should be a little over 1GB. If you expand the folder structure, you will find a folder with the current Office version number (at the time of writing, this is 15.0.4701.1002), which contains a number of `.cab` and `.dat` files.

8. To convert these files into the `.appv` format and save the result to the App-V package store, return to the command prompt and run the following command:

```
setup.exe /packager .\configuration.xml "\\demo.org\app-v\Office 2013"
```

9. After a short pause, this will launch another command window that reports the status of the packager:

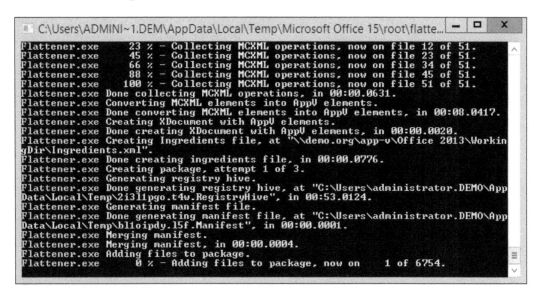

 By default, the progress report is also saved to the user's `temp` folder (which can be accessed by navigating to `%temp%` in the explorer) as a text document.

10. Once the packager has finished, navigate to `\\demo.org\app-v\Office 2013\AppVPackages` to find the generated `App-V` package and associated `.xml` configuration files.

# Enabling scripting and publishing in Office 2013

In order to run the Office 2013 package, the machine it is deployed to must have App-V scripting enabled (which is disabled by default as a security measure). To take advantage of the OS integration, the package must be deployed globally (to a machine security group instead of users).

## Getting ready

To complete these steps, you will need to complete the first recipe of this chapter and have access to a computer with the App-V client installed.

## How to do it...

The following list shows you the high-level steps involved in this recipe and the tasks required to complete the recipe (all of the actions in this recipe will take place on the server DC and a domain-joined Windows 8.1 computer):

- Enable scripting through Group Policy.
- Publish the Office 2013 package to domain computers.

The implementation of the preceding tasks is as follows:

1. On the server DC, open the Group Policy Management Console.
2. Expand the tree structure to show **Group Policy Objects | App-V 5 Settings**, right-click on **Group Policy Object** and click on **Edit...**.
3. In the window that appears, navigate to **Computer Configuration | Policies | Administrative Templates | System | App-V | Scripting**.
4. Double-click on **Enable Package Scripts Policy** and set the policy to **Enabled**. Click on **OK** to close the window.
5. On your Windows 8.1 computer, log in to the App-V Management Console (`http://appv1.demo.org:440/Console.html`) as Sam Adams.
6. Click on **ADD or UPGRADE PACKAGES**.
7. In the window that appears, set `\\demo.org\app-v\Office 2013\AppVPackages\ProPlusVolume_en-us_x86.appv` as the path to the App-V package and click on **Add**.
8. A window will then appear confirming that the application has been successfully imported, and you will see the package listed in the **Entire Library** pane.

9. To grant the domain computers security group the permission to access the application, right-click on the package and click on **edit active directory access**.

10. In the **FIND VALID ACTIVE DIRECTORY GROUPS AND GRANT ACCESS** box, enter `demo.org\Domain Computers` and then click on the **Check** button.

11. In the drop-down list that appears, select the **Domain Computers** group and then click on **Grant Access** to allow that group to access the package.

12. Note that the group is now added to the pane below the toolbar and that it uses the default configuration for that package.

13. Finally, to publish the package, right-click on the package and select **publish**.

# Customizing the Office 2013 App-V package

In the first recipe of this chapter, we looked at a very simple Office 2013 `configuration. xml` file that simply downloaded the 32-bit edition of Office 2013 Professional Plus. In this recipe, we will cover the process of including additional language packs and Office Visio 2013, as well as removing the Lync and OneDrive for Business applications.

## Getting ready

To complete these steps, you will need to complete the steps in the first recipe of this chapter.

## How to do it...

The following list shows you the high-level steps involved in this recipe and the tasks required to complete the recipe (all of the actions in this recipe will take place on the server `APPV1`):

▶ Create a custom `configuration.xml` file.

▶ Download the Office 2013 source files.

▶ Generate the Office 2013 package.

The implementation of the preceding tasks is as follows:

1. On the server APPV1, navigate to `C:\ODT` and create a copy of the current `configuration.xml` file, calling it `configurationwithvisio.xml`.

2. Right-click on the `configurationwithvisio.xml` file and select **Edit with Notepad++**.

3. Delete the default contents of the file and replace them with the following code snippet:

```
<Configuration>
  <Add SourcePath="\\demo.org\filestore\Office 2013 with
  Visio Source" OfficeClientEdition="32" >
    <Product ID="ProPlusVolume">
      <Language ID="en-us" />
      <Language ID="de-de" />
      <ExcludeApp ID="Lync" />
      <ExcludeApp ID="Groove" />
    </Product>
    <Product ID="VisioProVolume">
      <Language ID="en-us" />
      <Language ID="de-de" />
    </Product>
  </Add>
  <Property Name="PACKAGEGUID" Value="625f0332-a79c-4624-
  b90f-a8f415421cjb" />
</Configuration>
```

> The full list of language pack options can be found at the following link:
>
> `https://technet.microsoft.com/en-us/library/cc179219.aspx`
>
> The full list of applications that can be excluded can be found at the following link:
>
> `https://technet.microsoft.com/en-us/library/jj219426.aspx`
>
> Finally, the full list of product IDs can be found at this link:
>
> `https://technet.microsoft.com/en-gb/library/dn817830.aspx`

Let's take a look at the following screenshot:

```xml
configwithvisio.xml
1   <Configuration>
2     <Add SourcePath="\\demo.org\filestore\Office 2013 with Visio Source" OfficeClientEdition="32" >
3       <Product ID="ProPlusVolume">
4         <Language ID="en-us" />
5         <Language ID="de-de" />
6         <ExcludeApp ID="Lync" />
7         <ExcludeApp ID="Groove" />
8       </Product>
9       <Product ID="VisioProVolume">
10        <Language ID="en-us" />
11        <Language ID="de-de" />
12      </Product>
13    </Add>
14    <Property Name="PACKAGEGUID" Value="625f0332-a79c-4624-b90f-a8f415421cjb" />
15  </Configuration>
```

1. Note the following changes from the previous `configuration.xml` file after the modifications are done:

   - The source path is pointed to the `\\demo.org\filestore\Office 2013 with Visio Source` path

   - The German language is included by adding the extra `<Language ID="de-de" />` tags

   - Lync and OneDrive for Business (which is listed as Groove) is removed by using the `<ExcludeApp ID="Lync" />` and `<ExcludeApp ID="Groove" />` tags

   - The `VisioProVolume` parameter has been included in the `Product` tag

   - A `PACKAGEGUID` has been defined inside the `Property` tag. By default, the packager uses the same GUID for all Office 2013 packages; however, the App-V Management console must have a unique GUID for each package, thus you must define one here.

 To ensure that you use a unique GUID for each package, you can use the free tool available at `http://www.guidgenerator.com`.

2. Launch an administrative command prompt and run the following commands to change the directory to `C:\ODT`, and then begin the download process:

   ```
   cd C:\ODT

   setup.exe /download .\configurationwithvisio.xml
   ```

3. Once the download is complete, examine the file size of the `\\demo.org\` `filestore\Office 2013 with Visio Source` folder and expand the folder structure. You will find that the number of `.cab` and `.dat` files has increased, including the `stream.x86.de-de.dat` file, which contains the German language pack.

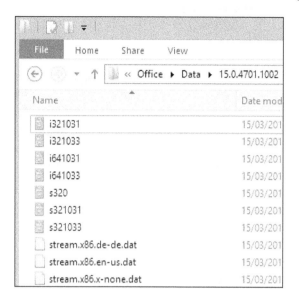

4. To convert these files into the `.appv` format and save the result to the App-V package store, return to the command prompt and run the following command:

   ```
   setup.exe /packager .\configurationwithvisio.xml "\\demo.org\
   app-v\Office 2013 with Visio"
   ```

5. Once the packaging process is complete, publish the package to the Domain Computers security group by using the steps in the second recipe of this chapter using `\\demo.org\app-v\Office 2013 with Visio\AppVPackages\` `VisioProVolume_ProPlusVolume_en-us_de-de_x86.appv` as the path to the App-V package.

**Office Visio and Project 2013**

You can only publish a single Office 2013 package to a security group of computers at any time; as such, you must include Visio or Project with the base Office package.

More information on this limitation can be found at `https://technet.microsoft.com/en-gb/library/` `dn817830.aspx#BKMK_deploy_visio_project`.

# Sequencing an Office 2013 plugin

By using Connection Groups, it is possible to sequence plugins for Office 2013. In this recipe, we will look at sequencing the Office Tabs plugin and then publishing it to our end users.

## Getting ready

To complete these steps, you will need to complete the first recipe of *Chapter 3, Sequencing Applications*, where you created a virtual machine to capture App-V packages.

## How to do it...

The following list shows you the high-level steps involved in this recipe and the tasks required to complete the recipe (all of the actions in this recipe will take place on the sequencing client called WIN8SEQUENCER):

- ▶ Download and extract the Office Tabs software.
- ▶ Install Office 2013 on the sequencing machine.
- ▶ Begin the sequencing process and capture the Office Tab plugin.
- ▶ Publish the Office Tab plugin.
- ▶ Reconfigure the Office Tab plugin to be compatible with your Office 2013 App-V package.
- ▶ Create a connection group and publish it to the end users.

The implementation of the preceding tasks is as follows:

1. Start WIN8SEQUENCER.
2. Visit http://www.extendoffice.com/download/office-tab.html and download the free version of Office Tab as an EXE and save it to C:\Temp.
3. Install Office 2013, apply any available updates, and then restart the computer.

 Note that this is the 'non virtualized' edition of Office 2013, for example, using the ISO downloaded from the Volume License Service Centre. Furthermore, it would be wise to take a snapshot of your virtual machine at this stage in the event that something goes wrong in the process of installing the plugin.

4. Launch the App-V Sequencer, accepting any **User Account Control Prompts** dialog by clicking on **Yes**.
5. Click on **Create a New Virtual Application Package**.

6. With **Create Package (default)** selected, click on **Next**.

7. Review any warnings about the current system state (correcting the issues listed where possible) and click on **Next**.

8. Select **Add-on or Plug-in** and click on **Next**.

9. With the select the **Installer for the application** radio button checked, click, browse, and navigate to the Office Tab installer, which you downloaded earlier, and then click on **Next**.

10. Tick the **I have installed the primary parent program** box and click on **Next**.

Install the primary parent program.

Before sequencing the add-on or plug-in, ensure that the primary parent program is installed on the machine. You can install the primary parent program by using one of the following methods:

1. Install the primary parent program to the machine.

2. Expand the primary parent program virtual application package to the machine. Note: This process may take a while.

Expand Package

Once you have installed the primary parent program, click the checkbox below to continue:

☐ I have installed the primary parent program.

11. Set the **Virtual Application Package Name** option as `Office Tab Plugin` and click on **Next**.

12. When you reach the **Install your applications now** screen, wait a moment for the Office Tab installer to appear; accept all of the default settings and install Office Tab to the default location.

13. Return to the App-V Sequencer, tick the **I am finished installing** box, and click on **Next**.

14. Review the **Installation Report** screen and click on **Next**.

15. With **Stop now** selected, click on **Next**.

16. Finally, accept the default save location for the package and click on **Create**.

17. Once the package is created, copy it to the `\\demo.org\app-v` file share.

18. On your Windows 8.1 computer, log in to the App-V Management Console (`http://appv1.demo.org:440/Console.html`) as `Sam Adams`.

19. Publish the `Office Tab Plugin` package application to the Domain Computer security group.

20. Next, navigate to `\\demo.org\app-v\Office Tab Plugin` and open the Office Tab `Plugin_DeploymentConfig.xml` file in Notepad++.

21. Locate the **COM Mode** tag and change the mode from **Isolated** to **Integrated**. In addition to this, set `OutOfProcessEnabled` and `InProcessEnabled` to `True` (if not already set).

22. Finally, locate the `Objects Enabled` tag and set it to `False`.

```
265    <COM Mode="Integrated">
266      <IntegratedCOMAttributes OutOfProcessEnabled="true" InProcessEnabled="true" />
267    </COM>
268    <!--
269
270    Objects
271
272    -->
273    <Objects Enabled="false" />
```

 Steps 21 and 22 are necessary to ensure that the connection group will run, as these settings must also match the ones in the Office App-V package.

23. Save your changes to the file and return to the App-V Management Console.

24. Right-click on the **Office Tab Plugin** package and select **edit default configuration**.

25. In the bottom pane, scroll down to and click on **Import and Overwrite this Configuration**.

26. In the window that appears, select the Office Tab `Plugin_DeploymentConfig.xml` file that you just modified and accept the overwrite confirmation dialog that appears.

27. In the App-V Management console, navigate to **Connection Groups**.

28. Create a new Connection Group and call it `Office and Tabs Plugin`.

29. Set the connected packages as the `Office 2013` package and the `Office Tab Plugin` package, and ensure that they are displayed in this order so that they are processed correctly on the client.

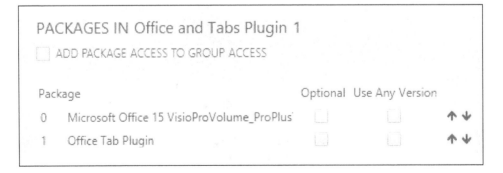

PACKAGES IN Office and Tabs Plugin 1

☐ ADD PACKAGE ACCESS TO GROUP ACCESS

| Package | | Optional | Use Any Version | |
|---|---|---|---|---|
| 0 | Microsoft Office 15 VisioProVolume_ProPlus | ☐ | ☐ | ↑ ↓ |
| 1 | Office Tab Plugin | ☐ | ☐ | ↑ ↓ |

30. Grant permission for the Domain Computers security group to access this connection group and publish the connection group.

31. To test the plugin, force an App-V Publishing refresh on your client computer, launch Microsoft Office Word, and verify that the tabs functionality has been added.

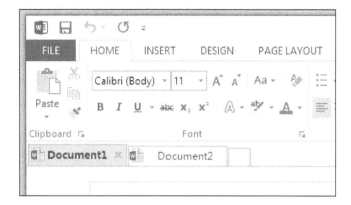

 If an Office package has already been launched on the client, it might be necessary to restart the computer before the functionality is included.

# 7

# Deploying App-V 5 in a Virtual Environment

In this chapter, we will cover:

- ▸ Enabling the App-V shared content store mode
- ▸ Publishing applications through Microsoft RemoteApp
- ▸ Precaching applications in the local store
- ▸ Publishing applications through **Citrix StoreFront**

## Introduction

App-V 5 is the perfect companion for your virtual session or desktop delivery environment, allowing you to abstract applications from the user and desktop, as shown in the following image, and, in turn, reducing infrastructure requirements through features such as **shared content store mode**.

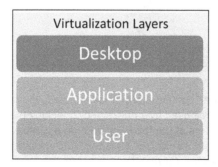

In this chapter, we will cover how to deploy App-V5 in these environments.

# Enabling the App-V shared content store mode

In this recipe, we will cover enabling the App-V shared content store mode, which prevents the caching of App-V files on a client so that the application is launched from the server hosting the application directly.

This feature is ideal for environments where there is ample network bandwidth between remote desktop session hosts (or client virtual machines in a VDI deployment) and where administrators are looking to reduce the overall need for storage by the hosts.

While some files are still cached on the local machine (for example, for shortcuts or Shell extensions), the following screenshot shows the amount of storage saved on an Office 2013 deployment, where the shared content store mode is turned on (the screenshot on the right):

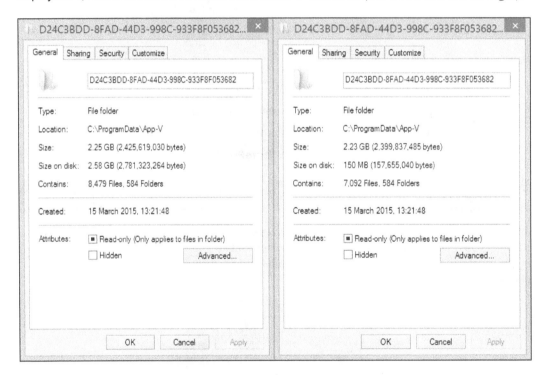

 With the shared content store mode enabled, you can check the amount of storage space used by a package by checking the size of the individual package's folders at the following path on a client where the package is deployed (where `Package ID` is the GUID assigned to that package): `C:\ProgramData\App-V\<Package ID>`.

## Getting ready

To complete these steps, you will need to complete the recipes in the first four chapters and deploy a Remote Desktop Services environment (on the server RDS).

The server RDS must also have the App-V client and any prerequisites deployed on it.

## How to do it...

The following list shows you the high-level tasks involved in this recipe and the tasks required to complete the recipe (all of the actions in this recipe will take place on the server DC):

- ▶ Link the App-V5 Settings Group Policy Object to the Remote Desktop Server's OU.
- ▶ Create a Group Policy object for the server RDS.
- ▶ Enable the shared content store mode within that policy.

The implementation of the preceding tasks is as follows:

1. On the server DC, load the Group Policy Management console.
2. Expand the tree structure to display the Remote Desktop Server's Organizational Unit and click on **Link an Existing GPO...**.
3. From the window that appears, select the **App-V 5 Settings** policy and click on **OK**.
4. Next, right-click on the OU and select **Create a GPO in this domain, and Link it here...**.
5. Set the name of the policy as App-V 5 Shared Content Store and click on **OK**. Let's take a look at the following screenshot:

6.  Right-click on the policy you have just created and click on **Edit...**.

7.  In the window that appears, right-click on **App-V 5 Shared Content Store** and click on **Properties**. Then, tick the **Disable User Configuration settings** box and click on **OK**.

8.  Next, navigate to **Computer Configuration | Policies | Administrative Templates | System | App-V | Streaming** and double-click on **Shared Content (SCS) mode**.

9.  Set the policy to **Enabled** and click on **OK**.

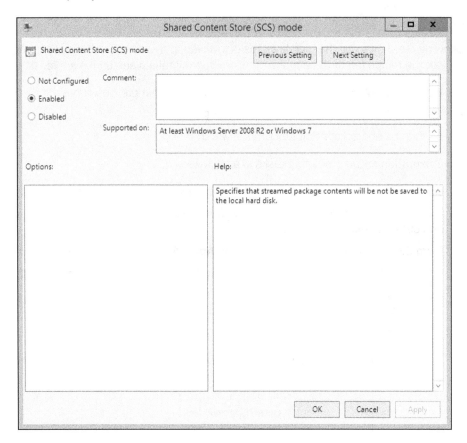

## There's more...

To verify that the setting is applied on the server RDS, open a PowerShell session and run the following command:

```
Get-AppvClientConfiguration
```

If the `SharedContentStoreMode` value is `1` and the `SetByGroupPolicy` value is `True`, then the policy is correctly applied.

# Publishing applications through Microsoft RemoteApp

In this recipe, we will publish the `Audacity` package created in *Chapter 3, Sequencing Applications*, to the `RDS` server to be accessed by users through the Remote Desktop Web Access.

## Getting ready

To complete these steps, you will need to complete the recipes in the first four chapters and deploy a Remote Desktop Services environment (on the server `RDS`).

## How to do it...

The following list shows you the high-level tasks involved in this recipe and the tasks required to complete the recipe (all of the actions in this recipe will take place on the server `RDS`):

- Create a Security Group for your remote desktop session hosts.
- Publish the `Audacity` package to that Security Group through the App-V Management console.
- Publish the `Audacity` package through Server Manager.

The implementation of the preceding tasks is as follows:

1. On the server `DC`, launch the Active Directory Users and Computers console and navigate to **demo.org | Domain Groups,** and create a new Security Group called `RDS Session Hosts`.

2. Add the server `RDS` to the group that you just created.

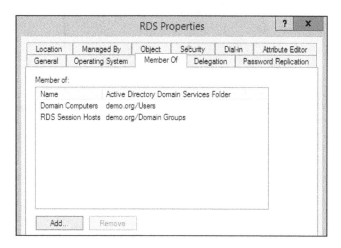

3. On your Windows 8 client PC, log in to the App-V Management console as Sam Adams, select the **Audacity** package and click on the **Edit** option next to the **AD ACCESS** option.

4. Under **FIND VALID ACTIVE DIRECTORY GROUP AND GRANT ACCESS**, enter demo.org\RDS Session Hosts and click on **Check**.

5. In the drop-down menu that appears, select **RDS Session Hosts** and click on **Grant Access**.

6. On the server RDS, wait for the App-V Publishing Refresh to occur (or force the process manually) for the **Audacity** shortcut to appear on the desktop.

7. Launch Server Manager, and from the left-hand side bar, select **Remote Desktop**.

8. From the left-hand side, select **QuickSessionCollection** (the collection created by default).

9. Under **REMOTEAPP PROGRAMS**, navigate to **Tasks** | **Publish RemoteApp Programs**.

10. In the window that appears, tick the box next to **Audacity** and click on **Next**, as shown in the following screenshot:

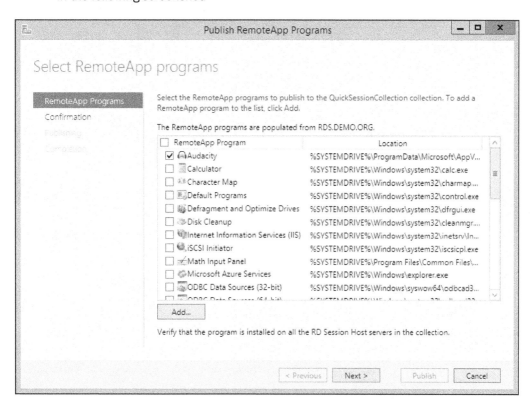

 Note that the path to the Audacity application is pointing at the App-V Installation root in %SYSTEMDRIVE%\ProgramData\Microsoft\AppV.

11. Review the confirmation window and click on **Publish**.

12. On your Windows 8 client, open Internet Explorer and browse to https://rds.demo.org/RDWeb, accepting any invalid SSL certificate prompts and allowing the Remote Desktop plugin to run.

13. Log in as `Sam Adams` and launch the `Audacity` application.

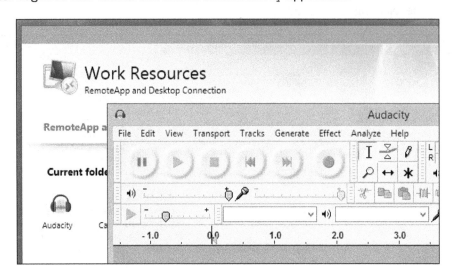

## There's more...

It is possible to limit applications within a remote desktop collection to users in a specific Security Group. To do this, right-click on the application as it appears under **REMOTEAPP PROGRAMS** and click on **Edit Properties**:

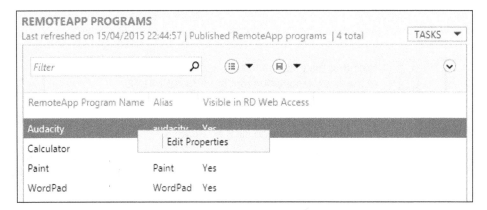

In the window that appears, click on **User Assignment** and set the radio button to **Only specified users and groups**. You will now be able to access the **Add...** button, which brings up an **Active Directory** search dialog, from where you can add the `Audacity Users` security group to limit the application to only the users in that group.

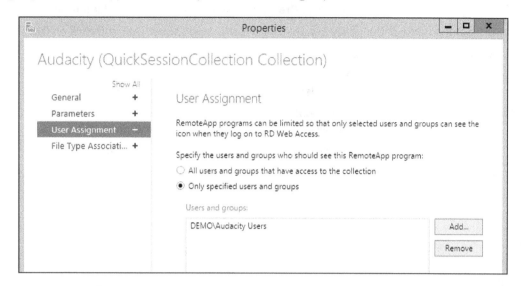

# Precaching applications in the local store

As an alternative to using the Shared Content Store mode, applications can be forced to be cached within the local store on your RDS session hosts. This would be advantageous in scenarios where the bandwidth from a central high speed storage device is more expensive than providing dedicated storage to the RDS session hosts.

## Getting ready

To complete these tasks, you will need to complete the recipes in the first four chapters and deploy a Remote Desktop Services environment (on the server RDS).

## How to do it...

The following list shows you the high-level tasks involved in this recipe and the tasks required to complete the recipe (all of the actions in this recipe will take place on the server DC):

  ▶ Create a group policy object for the server RDS.
  ▶ Enable background application caching within that policy.

The implementation of the preceding tasks is as follows:

1. On the server DC, load the Group Policy Management console.

2. Expand the tree structure to display **Remote Desktop Servers Organizational Unit**, right-click on the OU, and select **Create a GPO in this domain, and Link it here...**.

3. Set the name of the policy to App-V 5 Cache Applications and click on **OK**.

4. Right-click on the policy you have just created and click on **Edit...**.

5. In the window that appears, right-click on **App-V5 Cache Applications** and click on **Properties**, tick the **Disable User Configuration settings** box and click on **OK**.

6. Next, navigate to **Computer Configuration | Policies | Administrative Templates | System | App-V | Specify what to load in background (aka AutoLoad)**.

7. Set the policy to **Enabled**, with **Autoload Options** set to **All**, and click on **OK**.

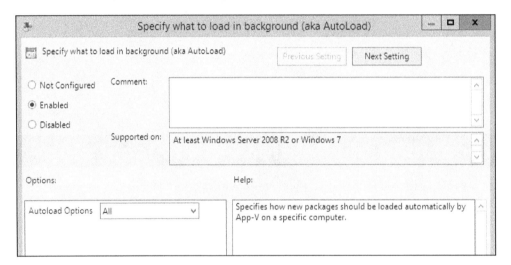

## There's more...

Individual applications can be targeted for caching using the Mount-AppvClientPackage PowerShell command. For example, to mount the package named Audacity 2.0.6 (which has been already published to the Remote Desktop session host), the administrator would run the following command:

```
Mount-AppvClientPackage -Name "Audacity 2.0.6"
```

This would generate the following result:

```
PS C:\Users\administrator.DEMO> Mount-AppvClientPackage -Name "Audacity 2.0.6"

PackageId              : 30f1b169-1fff-44fb-ba1f-3381d9a4caef
VersionId              : 223f13c9-c8de-4912-80db-61166ba5194e
Name                   : Audacity 2.0.6
Version                : 0.0.0.1
Path                   : \\demo.org\app-v\Audacity 2.0.6\Audacity 2.0.6.appv
IsPublishedToUser      : False
UserPending            : False
IsPublishedGlobally    : True
GlobalPending          : False
InUse                  : False
InUseByCurrentUser     : False
PackageSize            : 50463783
PercentLoaded          : 100
IsLoading              : False
HasAssetIntelligence   : True
```

Note that the **PercentLoaded** value is shown as **100** to indicate that the package is completely loaded within the local store.

# Publishing applications through Citrix® StoreFront

Apart from being a great addition to the Microsoft Virtual environment, App-V is also supported by **Citrix XenDesktop**. In this recipe, we will look at publishing the Audacity package through Citrix StoreFront.

## Getting ready

To complete these steps, you will need to complete the recipes in the first four chapters. In addition to this, the server XenDesktop and XD-HOST will be used in this recipe. XenDesktop is configured with an installation of XenDesktop 7.6 with a **Machine Catalogue** containing the server XD-HOST (configured as a Server OS Machine) and a delivery group that has been set up to service both applications and desktops.

The server XD-HOST should have the App-V RDS client installed. Finally, the App-V applications that you wish to deploy through Citrix StoreFront must also be published to the server XD-HOST through the App-V Management console; in this case, Audacity.

## How to do it...

The following list shows you the high-level steps involved in this recipe and the tasks required to complete the recipe (all of the actions in this recipe will take place on the server XenDesktop):

- ▸ Set up App-V Publishing in Citrix Studio.
- ▸ Publish applications through the Delivery Group.

The implementation of the preceding tasks is as follows:

1.  On the server XenDesktop, launch Citrix Studio.
2.  Navigate to **Citrix Studio | Configuration**, right-click on **App-V Publishing**, and click on **Add App-V Publishing**.

3. In the window that appears, enter the details of your App-V Management and Publishing servers, click on **Test connection...** to confirm that the details are correct and then click on **Save**.

4. Navigate to **Delivery Groups**, right-click on the delivery group you have created, and click on **Add Applications**.

5. On the introduction page of the wizard that appears, click on **Next**.

6. On the applications page of the wizard, select **Audacity** from the list provided (which will be discovered automatically from your server XD-HOST) and click on **Next**.

 Note that you can also select to publish multiple applications at the same time.

7. Review the summary screen and click on **Finish**.

## There's more...

Similar to publishing through the Microsoft remote desktop web app, it is possible to limit access to your applications to specific users or security groups. To limit access, right-click on your application in the **Applications** tab of the **Delivery Groups** page and click on **Properties**.

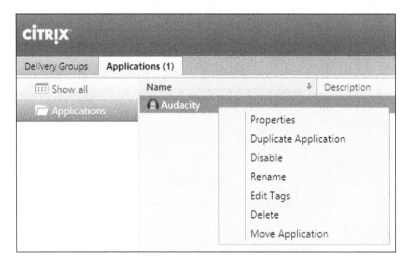

In the window that appears, select the **Limit Visibility** tab and select **Limit visibility for this application to the users listed below**. Click on the **Add users...** button to choose users and security groups from Active Directory to be included in the group.

# 8
# Managing Packages in System Center Configuration Manager 2012 R2

In this chapter, we will cover:

- ▸ Importing an App-V 5 package into SCCM 2012 R2
- ▸ Creating machine and user collections
- ▸ Targeting an App-V 5 package at a machine for deployment
- ▸ Targeting an App-V 5 package at a user for deployment
- ▸ Customizing the App-V package in SCCM
- ▸ Testing the packages
- ▸ Creating an App-V virtual environment

## Introduction

Administrators who already have a Microsoft **System Center Configuration Manager** (**SCCM**) infrastructure in place may wish to leverage it to deploy App-V packages instead of deploying a dedicated App-V infrastructure. Depending on the administrator's choices, SCCM also offers users the choice of applications to be installed on their PC through the Application Catalog.

The recipes in this chapter will show you how to leverage this infrastructure to deploy App-V packages. Note that both the SCCM client and App-V client are installed on all of the client PCs in this example and that there is no need to deploy an App-V Publishing server or to configure Group Policy for App-V.

# Importing an App-V 5 package into SCCM 2012 R2

In this recipe, we will cover the steps to import an App-V package into SCCM using the SCCM management console for deployment to clients.

## Getting ready

To complete these tasks, you will need to have a functioning SCCM infrastructure, as well as the `Audacity` and `VLC media player` packages created in the previous chapters. These packages are hosted on the `\\demo.org\App-V DFS` file share.

## How to do it...

The following list shows you the high-level steps involved in this recipe and the tasks required to complete the recipe (all of the actions in this recipe will take place on the server `SCCM`):

▸ Create a new folder in applications to store the packages.

▸ Import Audacity into SCCM.

▸ Import the VLC Media Player into SCCM.

The implementation of the preceding tasks is as follows:

1. On the server `SCCM`, launch the SCCM Management console.

2. Go to **Software Library** and navigate to **Application Management | Applications**.

3.  Right-click on **Applications**, select **Folder**, and then click on **Create Folder**.

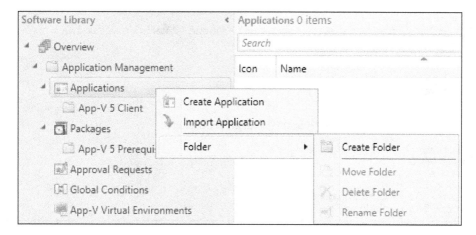

4.  In the window that appears, set the name of the folder to `App-V 5 Packages` and click on **OK**.

5.  Right-click on the folder you have just created and click on **Create Application**.

6.  In the window that appears, from the **Type** drop-down menu, select **Microsoft Application Virtualization 5**.

7.  Click on the **Browse** button and navigate to `\\demo.org\app-v\Audacity 2.0.6.` Select the `Audacity 2.0.6.appv` file in this folder and click on **Open**. Click on **Next**.

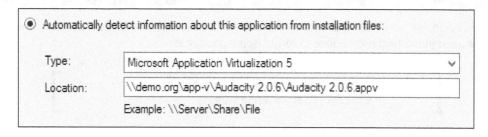

8. Review the **Imported Information** screen and click on **Next**.

 Application information successfully imported from the Microsoft Application Virtualization 5 file.

Details:

Application name: Audacity 2.0.6
Publisher:
Software version:
Deployment type name: Audacity 2.0.6 - Microsoft Application Virtualization 5

Content location: \\demo.org\app-v\Audacity 2.0.6
Number of files: 3
Content files:
    Audacity 2.0.6.appv
    Audacity 2.0.6_DeploymentConfig.xml
    Audacity 2.0.6_UserConfig.xml

9. On the **General Information** screen, specify any additional details as required (for example, adding an administrator's comment to list the name of the administrator who created the package) and click on **Next**.

10. Review the **Summary** screen and click on **Next**.

11. Finally, review the **Completion** screen and click on **Close**.

12. Repeat steps 5-12 for the VLC package.

# Creating machine and user collections

In this recipe, we will create a collection of machines and another collection of users, which will be used in the next two recipes to target App-V packages.

 Note that collections can only contain machines or users and not both at the same time.

## Getting ready

To complete these steps, you will need a functioning SSCM infrastructure and you should have created the `Audacity` applications as discussed in *Chapter 3, Sequencing Applications*.

## How to do it...

The following list shows you the high-level tasks involved in this recipe and the tasks required to complete the recipe (all of the actions in this recipe will take place on the server `SCCM`):

- ▸ Create the machine collection.
- ▸ Create the user collection.
- ▸ Add the testing client to the machine collection.
- ▸ Add the user `Sam Adams` to the user collection.

The implementation of the preceding tasks is as follows:

1. On the server `SCCM`, launch the SCCM Management console.

2. Navigate to **Assets and Compliance**, right-click on **Device Collections**, and click on **Create Device Collection**.

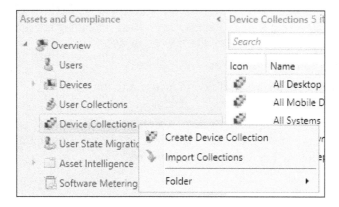

3. In the window that appears, set the name of the collection to `App-V 5 Desktop Clients` with the **Limiting collection** option set to **All Systems**. Click on **Next**.

4. On the **Membership Rules** screen, click on **Next**, accepting any prompts about no membership rules being defined by clicking on **OK**.

5. Review the **Summary** screen and click on **Next**.

6. On the **Completion** screen, click on **Close** to end the wizard.

7. On the **Assets and Compliance** tab, right-click on **User Collections** and click on **Create User Collection**.

8. In the window that appears, set the name of the collection to `App-V 5 Users` with the limiting collection option set to **All Users and User Groups**, click on **Next**.

9. On the **Membership Rules** screen, click on **Next**, accepting any prompts about no membership rules being defined by clicking on **OK**.

10. Review the **Summary** screen and click on **Next**.

11. On the **Completion** screen, click on **Close** to end the wizard.

12. To add the testing client (in this case, a domain-joined Windows 8.1 PC with the hostname `WIN8CLIENT`), navigate to **Assets and Compliance | Devices**. In the list of devices, right-click on your testing client and navigate to **Add Selected Items | Add Selected Items to Existing Device Collection**.

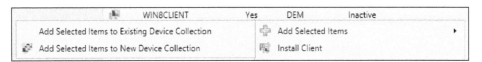

13. In the window that appears, set the **Collection** tab as the **App-V 5 Desktop Clients** collection that you created earlier and click on **OK**.

14. To add the user Sam Adams to the collection, navigate to **Assets and Compliance |** **Users**. In the list of users, right-click on Sam Adams and navigate to **Add Selected Items | Add Selected Items to Existing User Collection**.

15. In the window that appears, select the **App-V 5 Users** collection and click on **OK**.

> Both simple and complex rules can be defined to automatically add users and machines to collections. For more information on this, visit this Microsoft TechNet article at https://technet.microsoft.com/ en-us/library/gg712295.aspx.

# Targeting an App-V 5 package at a machine for deployment

In this recipe, we will target the VLC package that was imported earlier at the App-V 5 Desktop Clients collection.

## Getting ready

To complete these steps, you need a functioning SCCM infrastructure and you should have completed the first two recipes of this chapter.

## How to do it...

The following list shows you the high-level steps involved in this recipe and the tasks required to complete the recipe (all of the actions in this recipe will take place on the server SCCM):

▸ Deploy the VLC package.

The implementation of the preceding task is as follows:

1.  On the server SCCM, launch the SCCM Management console and navigate to
    **Software Library** | **Application Management** | **Applications** | **App-V 5 Packages**.

2.  Right-click on the **VLC** package that you imported earlier and click on **Deploy**.

3.  In the window that appears, click on the **Browse** button next to **Collection**, then the
    **Select Collection** window will appear. From the drop-down menu in the top-left pane,
    select **Device Collections**.

4.  In the list displayed, select the **App-V 5 Desktop Clients** collection and click on **OK**.
    Click on **Next**.

5. As this is the first time the package is being deployed and you need to distribute it to your SCCM distribution points, on the **Content** screen, click on the **Add** button and select **Distribution Point** from the drop-down menu.

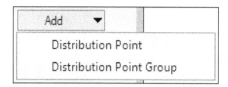

6. In the window that appears, tick the distribution point for the server SCCM.DEMO.ORG and click on **OK**. Click on **Next**.

7. On the **Deployment Settings** screen, set the **Action** option to **Install** and the **Purpose** option to **Required**. Click on **Next**.

At this stage, you can elect to send wake-up packets to any machine that is powered off and supports Wake on LAN in the selected collection. This is a great feature for overnight deployments of large packages that might impact end users if done during working hours.

8. Click on **Next** through the **Scheduling, User Experience** and **Alerts** screens.

9. Review the **Summary** screen and click on **Next**.

10. On the **Completion** screen, click on **Close** to end the wizard.

# Targeting an App-V 5 package at a user for deployment

In this recipe, we will target the Audacity 2.0.6 package that was imported earlier into the App-V 5 users collection for end users to opt for the installation through the Application Catalog.

## Getting ready

To complete these steps you will need to have a functioning SCCM infrastructure (including the Application Catalog roles) and should have completed the first two recipes of this chapter.

## How to do it...

The following list shows you the high-level steps involved in this recipe and the tasks required to complete the recipe (all of the actions in this recipe will take place on the server SCCM):

▸ Deploy the `Audacity 2.0.6` package.

The implementation of the preceding task is as follows:

1. On the server SCCM, launch the SCCM Management console and navigate to **Software Library | Application Management | Applications | App-V 5 Packages**.

2. Right-click on the **Audacity 2.0.6** package that you imported earlier and click on **Deploy**.

3. In the window that appears, click on the **Browse** button next to **Collection**, then the **Select Collection** window will appear. From the list displayed, select the **App-V 5 Users** collection and click on **OK**.

4. Click on **Next**.

5. As with the VLC package, this is the first time the package is being deployed and you need to distribute it to your SCCM distribution points. On the **Content** screen, click on the **Add** button and select **Distribution Point** from the drop-down menu.

6. In the window that appears, tick the distribution point for the server SCCM.DEMO.ORG and click on **OK**.

7. Click on **Next**.

8. On the **Deployment Settings** screen, set the **Action** option to **Install** and the **Purpose** option to **Available**.

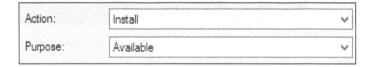

 Setting the **Purpose** option to **Required** will not give the user the choice to install the package, but it will be installed automatically instead.

9. Click on **Next**.

10. Click on **Next** through the **Scheduling, User Experience**, and **Alerts** screens.

11. Review the **Summary** screen and click on **Next**.

12. On the **Completion** screen, click on **Close** to end the wizard.

# Customizing the App-V package in SCCM

Through the SCCM Management console, it is possible to set the package to streaming instead of the local delivery mode in order to hide applications within a package from the user and to limit package publishing depending on the administrator-defined hardware or software requirements.

Note that, at this time, there is no way to modify the file type associations for App-V packages within SCCM.

## Getting ready

To complete these steps, you will need to have a functioning SCCM infrastructure and should have completed the *Importing an App-V 5 package into SCCM 2012 R2*, *Creating machine and user collections* and *Targeting an App-V 5 package at a machine for deployment* recipes of this chapter.

## How to do it...

The following list shows you the high-level steps involved in this recipe and the tasks required to complete this recipe (all of the actions in this recipe will take place on the server SCCM):

- ▶ Access the properties page for the VLC package.
- ▶ Set the package to the streaming mode instead of the local delivery mode.
- ▶ Hide all applications other than the VLC media player.
- ▶ Set a hardware requirement.

The implementation of the preceding tasks is as follows:

1. On the server SCCM, launch the SCCM Management console.
2. Navigate to **Software Library** | **Application Management** | **Applications** | **App-V 5 Packages**.
3. Select the VLC package you imported in step 1, and select **Deployment Types** from the bottom pane.

4. Right-click on the listed deployment type and click on **Properties**.

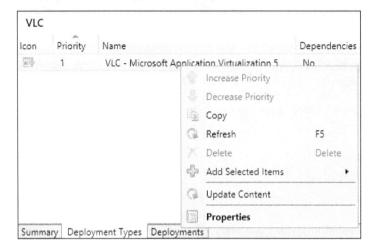

5. In the window that appears, select the **Content** tab. From the drop-down menu next to the **Deployment** options, select the **Stream content from distribution point** option.

In the streaming mode, the package will not be loaded onto the client until the user runs it for the first time. For more information on the advantages and disadvantages of the streaming and local delivery modes, visit the following link:

`https://technet.microsoft.com/en-gb/library/jj822982.aspx.`

6. Select the **Publishing** tab and remove the checkmark from all of the applications other than the VLC Media Player to prevent them from appearing on the user's **Start** menu or as a desktop icon.

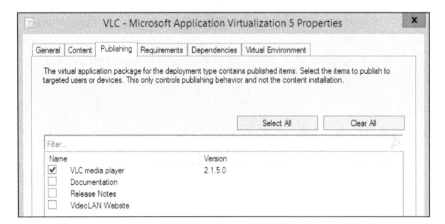

7. Select the **Requirements** tab and click on the **Add...** button.

8. To set the application to only run on clients with 2 GB or more of RAM, set the **Category** option to **Device**, the **Condition** option to **Total physical memory**, the **Rule type** option to **Value**, and the **Operator** option to **Greater than or equal to**. Also, set the **Value (MB)** option to 2048:

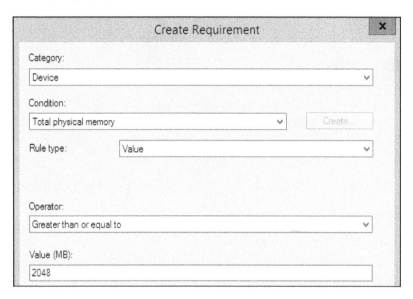

9. Click on **OK**.

10. Once you have finished making your changes to the package, click on **OK** to close the **Properties** window.

# Testing the packages

In this recipe, we will ensure that the VLC package is deployed to the machine's clients, and use the Application Catalog for the end user Sam Adams to choose to have the Audacity package deployed to his PC.

## Getting ready

To complete these steps, you will need to have a functioning SCCM infrastructure and should have completed the first four recipes of this chapter.

Note that applications will not deploy to clients until they have been distributed to the SCCM distribution servers. You can check on the progress of the distribution on the SCCM server by loading the SCCM Management console and navigating to **Monitoring | Distribution Status | Content Status**.

| Icon | Software | Type | Targeted | Size (MB) | Compliance % | Package ID |
|------|----------|------|----------|-----------|--------------|------------|
|  | Audacity 2.0.6 | Application | 1 | 28.63 | 100.0 | DEM00013 |
| | VLC | Application | 1 | 44.02 | 100.0 | DEM00014 |

## How to do it...

The following list shows you the high-level steps involved in this recipe and the tasks required to complete the recipe (all of the actions in this recipe will take place on your Windows 8.1 testing client):

- ▸ Verify that VLC has deployed to the client.
- ▸ Use the Application Catalog to install the Audacity package on to the client.

The implementation of the preceding tasks is as follows:

1. On the testing client, log in as Sam Adams.

2. Note that the VLC Media Player application is displayed on the desktop, proving that machine targeted deployment is working.

> If the VLC Player is not yet present on the desktop, you can force the SCCM client to update against the server by going to **Start | Control Panel | Configuration Manager | Actions** and running **Machine Policy Retrieval & Evaluation Cycle**.

3. From the **Start** menu, launch the **Software Center** application. Click on the **Find additional applications from the Application Catalog** link in the top right-hand corner.

4. In the window that appears, click on the Audacity package and click on **INSTALL**.

5. In the confirmation window that appears, click on **YES**.

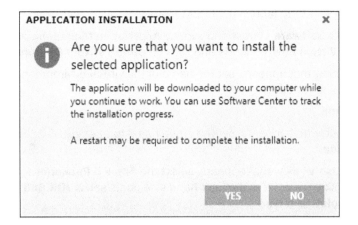

6. After a short pause, a notification will appear stating that the application's installation has started. Close the open window to return to the **Software Center** application.

7. From Software Center, you can monitor the progress of the installation. After a short pause, a window will appear stating that the installation is complete.

# Creating an App-V virtual environment

Virtual environments in SCCM are akin to Connection Groups in the App-V Management console and offer the same intra-package sharing of files and registry entries.

## Getting ready

To complete these steps, you will need to have a functioning SCCM infrastructure. In addition to this, you will need to have imported the JDK 8u31 and Greenfoot packages (created in the earlier chapters of this book) into SCCM using the instructions in the first recipe of this chapter.

## How to do it...

The following list shows you the high-level steps involved in this recipe and the tasks required to complete the recipe (all of the actions in this recipe will take place on the server SCCM):

▶ Create the Connection Group.

▶ Add the JDK 8u31 and Greenfoot packages to the connection group.

▶ Deploy the Greenfoot and JDK 8u31 packages to the machines.

The implementation of the preceding tasks is as follows:

1. On the server SCCM, launch the SCCM Management console.

2. Navigate to **Software Library** and expand **Application Management**. Now, right-click on **App-V Virtual Environments** and click on **Create Virtual Environment**.

3. In the window that appears, set the name of the virtual environment to `Greenfoot Connection Group`.

4. Click on **Add**.

5. In the window that appears, set the group name to `Prerequisites` and click on **Add**.

6. In the further window that appears, select the **App-V 5 Packages** folder from the left-hand side pane. From the right-hand side pane, select **JDK 8u31** and tick the **Listed deployment type**.

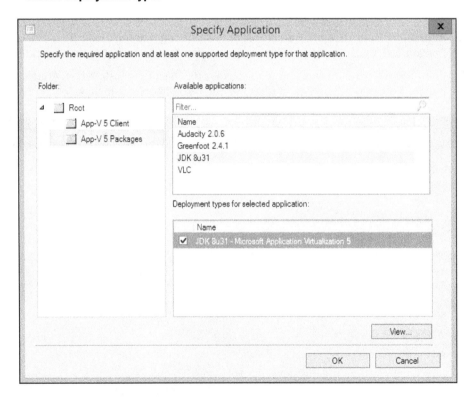

7. Click on **OK** and then click on **OK** again to close the **Add Applications** window.

8. In the **Create Virtual Environment** window, click on **Add** and repeat steps 5 through 7, this time adding the Greenfoot package into a Group called Greenfoot, as shown in the following screenshot:

9. Finally, deploy both the JDK 8u31 and Greenfoot packages to the App-V 5 Desktop Clients collection using the instructions in the recipe *Targeting an App-V 5 package at a machine for deployment*, of this chapter.

# 9
# Reporting in App-V 5

In this chapter, we will cover:

- ▸ Deploying the App-V 5 Reporting Server
- ▸ Configuring client-side settings through Group Policy
- ▸ Exporting reporting data into Excel 2013
- ▸ Analyzing reporting data in Excel 2013

## Introduction

App-V 5 provides a SQL-based logging database that includes information about users, the applications they use, and the machines they use them on. A key advantage of the reporting server is that it can be used regardless of the deployment method of the App-V package.

## Deploying the App-V 5 Reporting Server

In this recipe, we will cover the installation of the App-V reporting server (co-hosted with the App-V Management and Publishing Server that we set up in *Chapter 1, Deploying App-V 5 Services*) which will act as the repository of the reporting data.

## Getting ready

To complete these steps, you will need to complete the recipe *Deploying a Standalone Management and Publishing Server* in *Chapter 1, Deploying App-V 5 Services*.

The App-V Reporting Server can also be hosted as a standalone system; ensure that you install the prerequisites listed in the *Deploying a Standalone Management and Publishing Server* recipe of *Chapter 1, Deploying App-V 5 Services*, before starting the installation.

## How to do it...

The following list shows you the high-level steps involved in this recipe and the tasks required to complete the recipe (all of the actions in this recipe will take place on the server APPV1):

- ▸ Create the App-V Reporting Users Security Group and assign users to it
- ▸ Install the Reporting Server feature and database
- ▸ Configure SQL server permissions to allow the App-V Reporting Users Security Group to access the data
- ▸ Configure Windows Firewall to allow on the server DC

The implementation of the preceding tasks is as follows:

1. On the server APPV1, log in as an administrator, mount the App-V ISO, and run the sever installer.
2. Once the setup launches, click on **Install**.
3. On the **Getting Started** screen, review the software license terms, select the **I accept the license terms** radio button and click on **Next**.
4. On the **Update** screen, leave **Use Microsoft Update when I check for updates** checked and click on **Next**.

5. On the **Feature Selection** screen, tick the **Reporting Server** and **Reporting Server DB** checkboxes and click on **Next**, as shown here:

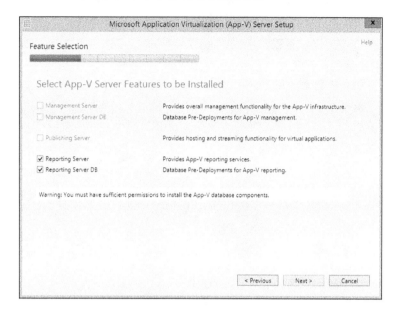

6. On the **Installation Location** screen, leave the default location as displayed and click on **Next**.

7. On the first **Configure** screen, leave the defaults for the **SQL Server instance** and **Reporting Server database** as displayed, and click on **Next**.

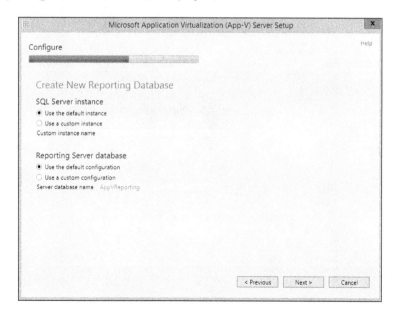

8. On the second **Configure** screen, leave the defaults as displayed and click on **Next**.

9. On the third and final **Configure** screen, take note of the website name and set the port number to 442. Now, click on **Next**.

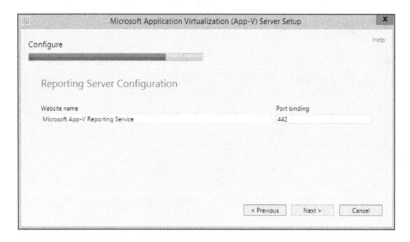

10. Review the **Ready** screen and click on **Next**.

11. Once the installation is complete, click on **Close**.

12. Launch services.msc and ensure that the **SQLSERVERAGENT** service is running and has its start up type set to **Automatic**, as shown here:

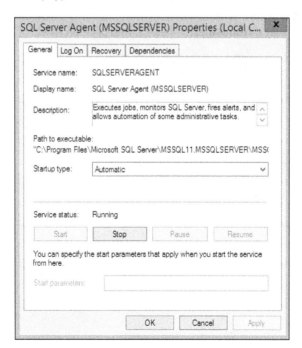

To ensure that the service can perform its tasks correctly, ensure that the **Log On** account is set as `NT SERVICE\SQLSERVERAGENT`.

This account is created by the SQL server installer and has access to the necessary permissions to securely run jobs on the SQL server. Alternatively, you may wish to create your own account for this purpose; details on the necessary permissions can be found in the MSDN article available at `https://msdn.microsoft.com/en-us/library/ms191543(v=sql.110).aspx`.

13. Launch **SQL Server Management Studio** and connect to the default instance on the server `APPV1`.

14. Expand **Security**, right-click on **Logins**, and select **New Login...**.

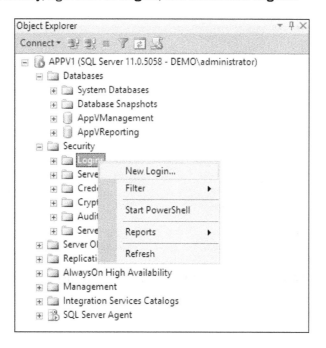

15. Set the **Login name** as **DEMO\App-V Reporting Users** and click on **OK**.

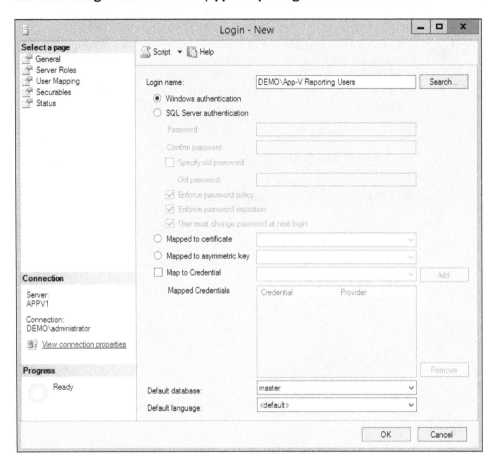

16. Now, expand **Databases** | **AppVReporting** | **Security**, right-click on **Users**, and select **New User...**.

17. Set the **User type** to **Windows user** and set the **User name** and **Login name** to **Demo\App-V Reporting Users**. Click on **OK**.

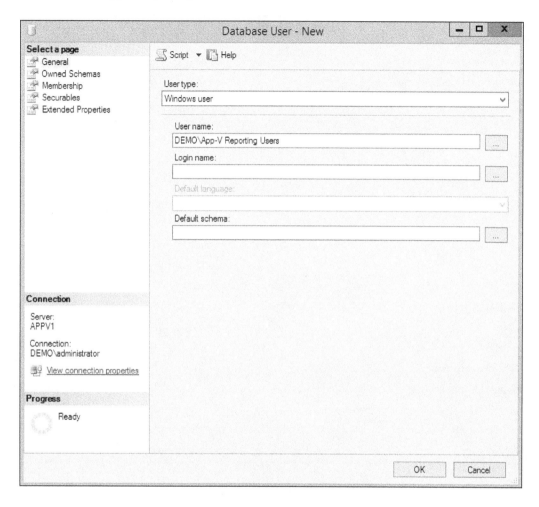

18. To allow access to only the **ApplicationUsage** and **ClientInformation** tables, navigate to **Databases | AppVReporting | Tables**.

19. Right-click on **dbo.ApplicationUsage** and click on **Properties**.

20. In the left-hand pane, select **Permissions**.

21. Next to **Users or roles**, click on the **Search...** button.

22. In the window that appears, enter **DEMO\App-V Reporting Users** and click on **Check Names**. Note that square brackets are applied to the security group to indicate that it is a valid group. Click on **OK**.

23. In the bottom-right pane, scroll down and tick the **Grant** box for the **Select** permission. Click on **OK**.

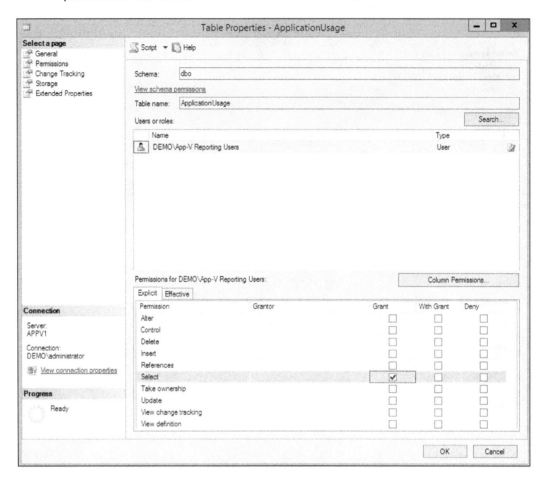

24. Repeat steps 19 to 23 for **dbo.ClientInformation**.

25. Finally, launch **Windows Firewall** with **Advanced Security**.

26. Right-click on **Inbound Rules** and click on **New Rule...**.

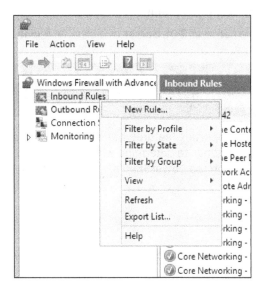

27. Set the rule type as **Port** and click on **Next**.
28. Leave the **TCP** option selected and set the port number to `1433`. Now, click on **Next**.

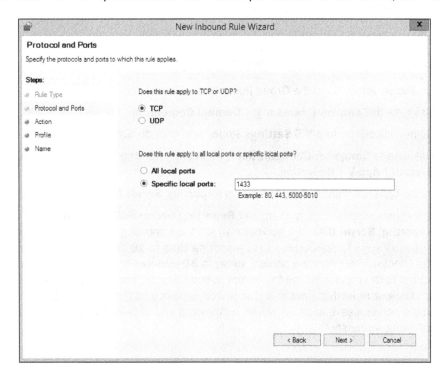

29. Leave the action as **Allow the connection** and click on **Next**.

30. Set the rule to only apply to the **Domain profile** and click on **Next**.

31. Finally, set the rule name as **SQL Server** and click on **Finish**.

# Configuring client-side settings through Group Policy

The App-V client includes the reporting features without any additional installation; however, it must be provided with the settings to determine where to send the reporting data. These settings can be provided through the **PowerShell** script or, as shown here, centrally through Group Policy.

## Getting ready

To complete these steps, you will need to complete the recipes in the first four chapters.

## How to do it...

The following list shows you the high-level steps involved in this recipe and the tasks required to complete the recipe (all of the actions in this recipe will take place on the server DC):

▶ Edit the App-V 5 Settings Group Policy object to include reporting server settings

The implementation of the preceding task is as follows:

1. On the server DC, load the Group Policy Management console.

2. Navigate to **Domains | demo.org | Domain Computers**.

3. Right-click on the **App-V 5 Settings Policy** and click on **Edit....**

4. Navigate to **Computer Configuration | Policies | Administrative Templates | System | App-V | Reporting**.

5. In the right-hand pane, double-click on **Reporting Server Policy**.

6. In the new window that appears, set **Reporting Server Policy** to **Enabled**, **Reporting Server URL** (the server on which the Reporting Server is configured) to `http://appv1.demo.org:442`, **reporting time** to **10** (the hour of the day at which the client will report to the server), **delay** to **30 minutes** (a random delay that is added to the reporting time to prevent overloading the reporting server), and finally, set **Repeat reporting time** to **1** (the period in days that the client will take to report to the server. Leave all other values as they are and click on **OK**, as shown in the following screenshot:

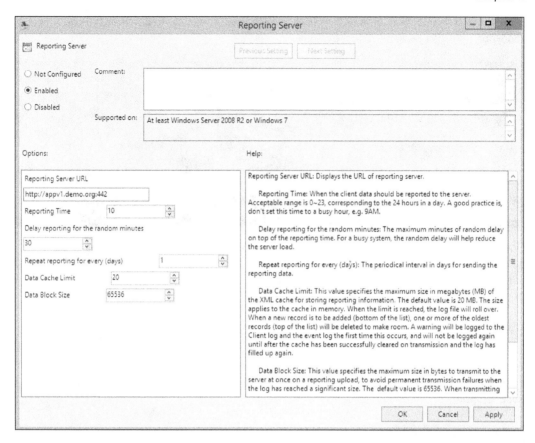

## There's more...

Once the policy has been applied to the client, it is possible to send the client report on demand by executing the following PowerShell commands as an administrator:

```
Import-Module AppvClient
Send-AppvClientReport
```

Once the command completes, PowerShell will display a message to confirm that the reporting data has been sent successfully:

```
                                              Administrator: Windows PowerShell
Windows PowerShell
Copyright (C) 2014 Microsoft Corporation. All rights reserved.

PS C:\Windows\system32> Import-Module AppvClient
PS C:\Windows\system32> Send-AppvClientReport
The Application Virtualization Client Report was sent successfully.
PS C:\Windows\system32> _
```

# Exporting reporting data into Excel 2013

Once the reporting data has been uploaded to the server, it is stored in a 'staging table' until a SQL Server Agent job dumps the data into the live tables. With this data stored in the SQL server, it is possible to view it through a variety of means, including custom designed websites and in Microsoft Office Excel.

## Getting ready

To complete these steps, you will need to complete the first two recipes of this chapter ensuring that the user Maddy Alans has been added to the App-V Reporting Users security group.

## How to do it...

The following list shows you the high-level steps involved in this recipe and the tasks required to complete the recipe (all of the actions in this recipe will take place on the server APPV1 and on a Windows 8.1 client running Office 2013):

▶ Manually execute the SQL Server Agent job to process the client data

▶ Create a connection to the SQL Server in Excel

The implementation of the preceding steps is as follows:

1. On the server APPV1, log in as an Administrator, launch the SQL Server Management Studio, and connect to the default instance on the server APPV1.

2. Navigate to **APPV1 | SQL Server Agent | Jobs**, right-click on the job **ProcessAppVReportingDataJob** and click on **Start Job at Step...**, as shown in the following screenshot:

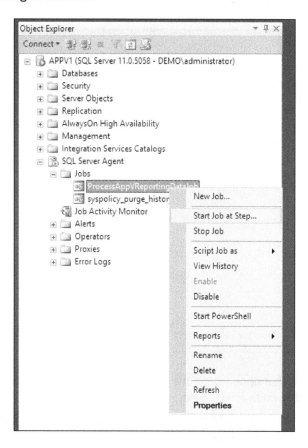

3. Wait for the process to complete.

4. On the Windows 8.1 client, log in as `Maddy Alans` and launch Microsoft Office Excel 2013.

5.  Browse to the **DATA** tab, click on the **From Other Sources** drop-down menu and select **From SQL Server**.

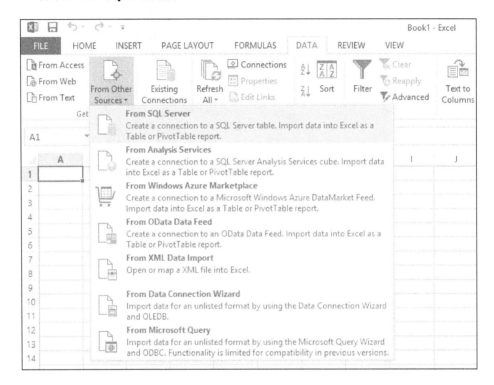

6.  In the window that appears, set the **Server name** as **APPV1 using Windows Authentication** and click on **Next**.

7.  Set the database to **AppVReporting** and tick the **Connect to a specific table** and **Enable selection of multiple tables** checkboxes.

8. From the tables below the checkboxes, tick the **ApplicationUsage** and **ClientInformation** tables, and click on **Next**.

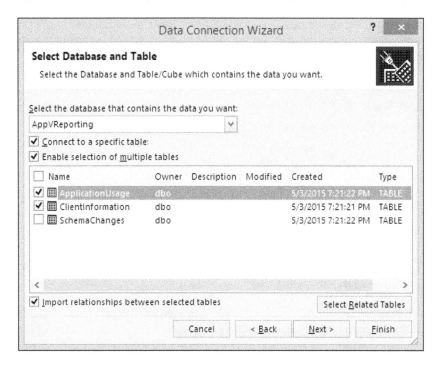

9. Accept the defaults for the **Save Data Connection File** and the **Finish** screen and click on **Finish**.

10. On the **Import Data** screen, select **Table** as the method of displaying the data and click on **OK**. This will then import the data from both tables and display them in two additional sheets.

With this data connection now set up, it will be possible to call it later without having to follow the steps outlined here by navigating to **DATA | Existing Connections** and selecting the saved connection.

# Analyzing reporting data in Excel 2013

With the data now in Excel, it is possible to use a **Pivot Table** to obtain meaningful insights into how applications are being used and the versions of the App-V client that are currently being used.

## Getting ready

To complete these steps, you will need to complete all of the recipes in this chapter.

## How to do it...

The following list shows you the high-level steps involved in this recipe and the tasks required to complete the recipe (all of the actions in this recipe will take place on a Windows 8.1 client running Office 2013.):

> ▸ Create a Pivot Table based on the application usage data

The implementation of the preceding task is as follows:

1. After importing the data into Excel as per the steps in the previous recipe, browse to the sheet containing the application usage data.
2. Select a cell within the table, navigate to the **INSERT** ribbon tab, and select **PivotTable**.
3. In the window that appears, set **PivotTable** to appear in a new worksheet and click on **OK**.

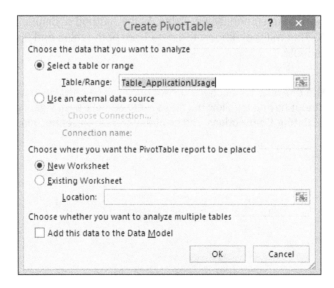

4. From the new sheet, select the **ANALYZE** ribbon tab and navigate to **Fields, Items & sets | Calculated Field...**.

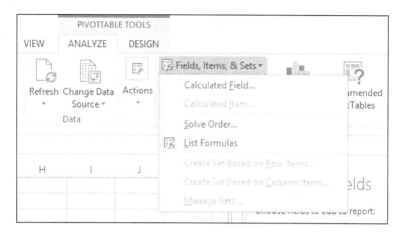

5. In the window that appears, set the name of the column as **Total time in use** and the formula as *=end_time - start_time*, and click on **Add**. With the formula added, click on **OK**.

6. This will automatically add the **Total time in use** value to **PivotTable**; however, it will not display it in any useable form. To change the formatting of this value, left-click on **Sum of Total time in use** under the **VALUES** header, and click on **Number Format** in the window that appears.

7. In the **Format Cells** window that appears, set **Format Type** to **hh:mm:ss** and click on **OK**. Click on **OK** again to return to the sheet and note that the value displayed in the Pivot Table now lists the hours, minutes, and seconds that all of the App-V applications in the database have been in use for.

8. To separate this time by application, drag the **app_name** field into the **ROWS** header.

| | Row Labels | Sum of Total time in use |
|---|---|---|
| 2 | | |
| 3 | **Row Labels** ▾ | **Sum of Total time in use** |
| 4 | Audacity | 00:03:35 |
| 5 | Excel 2013 | 00:55:44 |
| 6 | Greenfoot | 00:00:03 |
| 7 | VLC media player | 00:01:51 |
| 8 | Word 2013 | 00:03:41 |
| 9 | PowerPoint 2013 | 00:01:16 |
| 10 | **Grand Total** | **01:06:10** |
| 11 | | |
| 12 | | |

9. To further separate the data by user, drag the **username** field into the **ROWS** header.

10. To integrate the data to only show a specific date range, navigate to the **ANALYZE** ribbon tab and select **Insert Timeline**. From the window that appears, tick both the **start_time** and **end_time** fields and click on **OK**.

11. Using the timelines that appear, select a single day or a range of days to investigate.

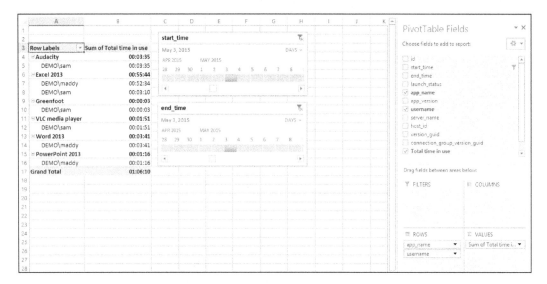

12. By reordering the **ROWS** header to have **username** above **app_name**, you can see the applications that your users have been using.

13. Finally, by displaying only the **app_name** field in the **ROWS** header and by setting the value to **Count of id**, you can see how many times a specific application has been launched.

14. A similar analysis can be performed against the **ClientInformation** table, where the **ROWS** groups are set to **os_type** and the version with **VALUES** is set to a count of **os_type**, in order to display the versions of App-V that are currently in use within the environment.

## There's more...

If you find that Excel displays an invalid value for the **Total time in use**, it may be possible that a user had an application open at the time the reporting data was sent (thus, there is no end time to compute the total time in use). To counter the effects of this invalid data, drag the **end_time** field into the **FILTERS** heading.

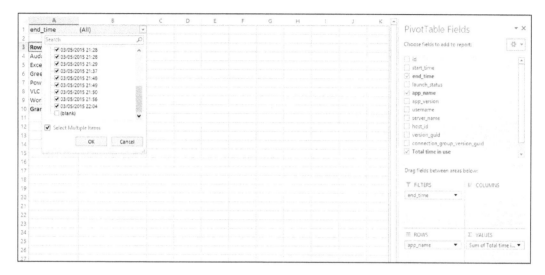

Using the **end_time** filter that is now displayed in **PivotTable,** click the drop down arrow and untick **blank** to exclude the invalid data from the table.

# 10
# Troubleshooting

In this chapter, we will cover:

- ▶ Analyzing server-side logs
- ▶ Analyzing client-side logs
- ▶ Laptops that don't pick up new applications
- ▶ Flushing the App-V client cache
- ▶ Checking the list of publishing packages for the user

## Introduction

Even with the most robust infrastructure you will likely have to troubleshoot issues with App-V at some point in your deployment. The recipes in this chapter will take you through the steps required to access the extensive App-V logging features, as well as solve some common issues.

## Analyzing server-side logs

As of App-V 5 SP3, server- and client-side logging is consolidated into the event log feature of Windows, and not all of the logging is exposed by default. In this recipe, you will learn how to enable and analyze these additional logs.

## Getting ready

To complete these steps, you will need to complete the recipes in *Chapter 1, Deploying App-V 5 Services*.

## How to do it...

The following list shows you the high-level steps involved in this recipe and the tasks required to complete this recipe (all of the actions in this recipe will take place on the server APPV1):

- ▶ Launch Event Viewer and view the App-V logs
- ▶ Enable Analytic and Debug logging

The implementation of the preceding tasks is as follows:

1. On the server APPV1, launch **Event Viewer** from the **Start** menu.

2. Navigate to **Applications and Services Logs** | **Microsoft** | **AppV**. Note the Server Management, Server-Publishing, and Server-Reporting folders that contain the default logs.

3. To show the additional logs, click on **View** | **Show Analytic and Debug Logs**.

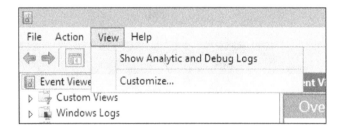

4. Additional log folders will then be displayed, including Server-Management-Private, Server-Publishing-Private, and Server-Reporting-Private; each log in these additional folders must be enabled individually.

5. To enable a log, right-click on it and click on **Enable Log**. The following example shows the **Analytic** log for **Server-Reporting-Private**:

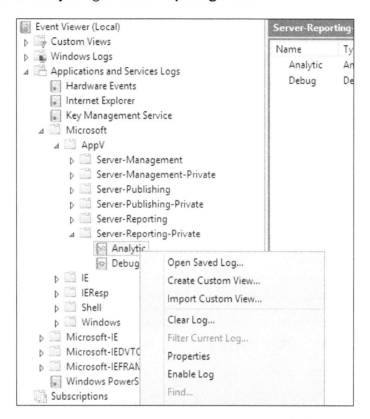

6. Click on **OK** to confirm that you want to enable the log. The following example shows the event logs captured when conducting a reporting server sync against a single client:

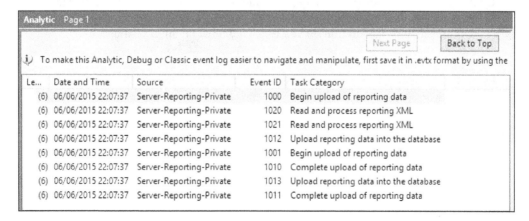

| Le... | Date and Time | Source | Event ID | Task Category |
|---|---|---|---|---|
| (6) | 06/06/2015 22:07:37 | Server-Reporting-Private | 1000 | Begin upload of reporting data |
| (6) | 06/06/2015 22:07:37 | Server-Reporting-Private | 1020 | Read and process reporting XML |
| (6) | 06/06/2015 22:07:37 | Server-Reporting-Private | 1021 | Read and process reporting XML |
| (6) | 06/06/2015 22:07:37 | Server-Reporting-Private | 1012 | Upload reporting data into the database |
| (6) | 06/06/2015 22:07:37 | Server-Reporting-Private | 1001 | Begin upload of reporting data |
| (6) | 06/06/2015 22:07:37 | Server-Reporting-Private | 1010 | Complete upload of reporting data |
| (6) | 06/06/2015 22:07:37 | Server-Reporting-Private | 1013 | Upload reporting data into the database |
| (6) | 06/06/2015 22:07:37 | Server-Reporting-Private | 1011 | Complete upload of reporting data |

The **Analytic and Debug** logging should not be enabled for protected periods on production systems as they can be filled with a significant quantity of data very quickly.

# Analyzing client-side logs

Just like in server-side logging, the App-V logs are consolidated in Event Viewer, and not all of the logging features are enabled by default. In this recipe, you will learn how to enable and analyze these additional logs.

## Getting ready

To complete these steps, you will need to have the App-V client installed on a Windows 8.1 PC.

## How to do it...

The following list shows you the high-level steps involved in this recipe and the tasks required to complete this recipe (all of the actions in this recipe will take place on the server DC):

▸ Launch Event Viewer and view the App-V logs
▸ Enable Analytic and Debug logging

The implementation of the preceding tasks is as follows:

1. On your Windows 8.1 client, launch **Event Viewer**.
2. Navigate to **Applications and Services Logs | Microsoft | AppV | Client** and note the **Admin**, **Operational** and **Virtual Applications** logs, which are enabled by default.
3. To show the additional logging, navigate to **View | Show Analytic and Debug Logs**.
4. A significant quantity of additional log folders will now be displayed. To gain greater insights into Client Reporting, for example, expand **Client-Reporting**, right-click on the **Debug** log, and click on **Enable Log** (each log must be enabled individually).

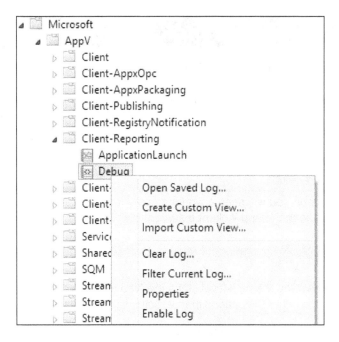

5. Click on **OK** to confirm that you want to enable the log.

6. The following example shows the result of the log from a failed upload of data to the reporting server (in this example, the reporting server was offline):

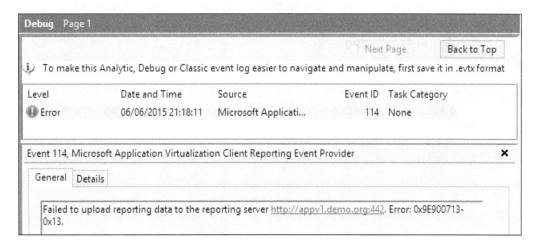

 The **Analytic and Debug** logging should not be enabled for protected periods on production systems as they can very quickly fill with a significant quantity of data.

# Laptops that don't pick up new applications

When using Group Policy to deploy App-V 5 settings, you will find that laptops or PCs that are running off batteries do not poll the App-V Publishing server for new applications. This common issue is caused by the Scheduled Task (which is created by Group Policy) not being set to run if the PC is not on AC power. A simple solution to this issue is to create your own Scheduled Task and deploy it through Group Policy client-side extensions.

## Getting ready

To complete these steps, you will need a working App-V infrastructure and a laptop or a PC running Windows 8.1 with the App-V client installed.

## How to do it...

The following list shows you the high-level steps involved in this recipe and the tasks required to complete this recipe (all of the actions in this recipe will take place on the server DC.):

▸ Create a Group Policy object for your Scheduled Task

The implementation of the preceding task is as follows:

1. On the server DC, launch the Group Policy Management console.
2. Expand **demo.org** and right-click on **Domain Computers**. Select **Create a GPO** in this domain, and click on **Link it here...**.
3. Set the name of the **GPO** as App-V 5 Laptop Settings.
4. Right-click on the newly created policy and click on **Edit...**.
5. In the window that appears, right-click on the policy and select **Properties**.
6. Place a mark in the checkbox next to the **Disable User Configuration** settings, accept any information dialogs, and click on **OK**.

7. Navigate to **Computer Configuration | Preferences | Control Panel Settings**, right-click on **Scheduled Tasks**, and go to **New | Scheduled Task (At least Windows 7)**.

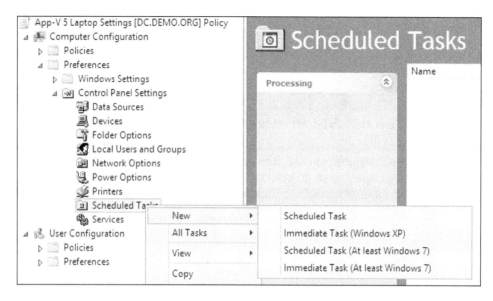

8. In the new window that appears, set **Action** to **Create**, **Name** to **Update App-V**, and the account to run the task as **BUILTIN\Users**, as shown in the following screenshot:

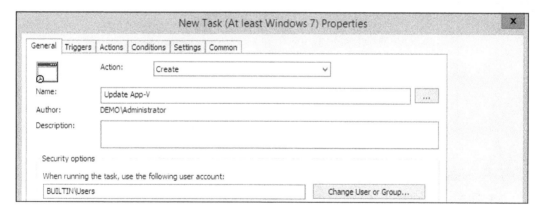

9. Navigate to the **Triggers** tab and click on **New...**.

10. In the window that appears, set **Begin the task** to **At log on** and click on **OK**:

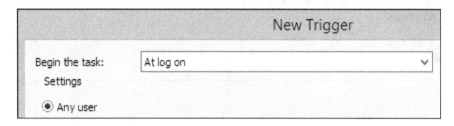

11. Navigate to the **Actions** tab and click on **New…**.

12. In the window that appears, set **Action** to **Start a program**, **Program/script** to **SyncAppvPublishingServer.vbs**, **Add arguments(optional)** as **1** (this will sync the first App-V publishing server as defined in Group Policy), and the **Start in(optional)** field as **C:\Program Files\Microsoft Application Virtualization\Client\**. Click on **OK**.

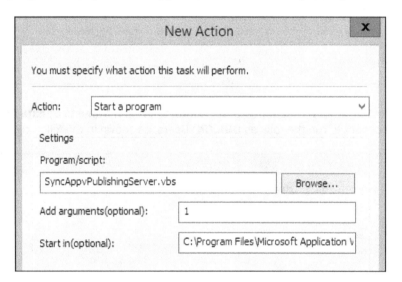

13. Navigate to the **Conditions** tab and ensure that the **Start the task only if the computer is on AC power** box is unchecked.

14. Finally, click on **OK** to finish creating the Scheduled Task.

# Flushing the App-V client cache

When creating a base operating system image for deployment to computers, you may wish to include the App-V client (to save deploying it through other means). However, if you launch an App-V application by mistake (before capturing the image), you might find that the package is included in the capture and thus bloats the image unnecessarily. By flushing the App-V client cache before capturing, you can ensure that no packages are included in the image.

## Getting ready

To complete these steps, you will need to have the App-V client installed on a Windows 8.1 PC.

## How to do it...

The following list shows you the high-level steps involved in this recipe and the tasks required to complete the recipe (all of the actions in this recipe will take place on the Windows 8.1 client):

- Log in as an `Administrator` and flush the App-V Client Cache

The implementation of the preceding task is as follows:

1. On your Windows 8.1 client, log in with an account that has local administrator permissions.

2. Launch an administrative PowerShell session and enter the following commands:

   ```
   Set-ExecutionPolicy RemoteSigned -Force

   Import-Module AppvClient

   Get-AppvClientPackage -All | Remove-AppvClientPackage

   Set-ExecutionPolicy Default -Force
   ```

   Here, the first and last lines of the commands allow scripting to run within PowerShell and then set the scripting security settings back to their default. The second line imports the App-V commands into the PowerShell session and the third line retrieves a list of all of the App-V packages and then pipes them into a command to remove them from the client.

3. To verify that the command has completed successfully, examine the size of the `C:\ProgramData\App-V` folder; it should be nearly empty with only icons and shortcuts remaining for the packages that have otherwise been cleared.

# Checking the list of publishing packages for the user

To verify the list of packages assigned to a user when using the App-V Publishing server infrastructure, an end user can visit the publishing server's address in a web browser to view the XML document created by the publishing server. This can be particularly useful when checking whether the packages have been correctly assigned to user groups.

## Getting ready

To complete these steps, you will need to have deployed an App-V Publishing server infrastructure and have the App-V client installed on a Windows 8.1 PC.

## How to do it...

The following list shows you the high-level steps involved in this recipe and the tasks required to complete the recipe (all of the actions in this recipe will take place on your Windows 8.1 client):

▶ Visit the App-V Publishing Server URL in a web browser

The implementation of the preceding task is as follows:

1. On your Windows 8.1 client, log in as a user that has App-V packages assigned to them. Open Internet Explorer and navigate to `http://app-vpublishing.demo.org:441`.

2. If prompted for authentication, enter your user's credentials.

3. Once the page loads, it will display the list of packages assigned against that user in the XML format; refer to the following example where the VLC Media Player package is assigned to the user:

# Index

Distributed File System Replication (DFS-R) 8

# E

**Electronic Software Distribution** 2
**Excel 2013**
reporting data, analyzing 178-181
reporting data, exporting 174-176

# F

**file type associations**
managing 93-95

# G

**Greenfoot**
about 108
sequencing 109, 110
URL 108
**Group Policy**
client-side settings, configuring 172-174
used, for applying settings to
App-V client 58-61
used, for deploying App-V client 44-47
used, for deploying App-V client
updates 50-53
**Group Policy Object (GPO)** 4
**GUID**
URL 124

# I

**Internet Explorer shortcut**
sequencing 72-74
**Internet information services (IIS)**
about 13
configuring 14-21

# J

**Java Development Kit (JDK)**
about 106
sequencing 106-108

# L

**language pack options**
URL 123

# M

**machine**
App-V 5 package, targeting for
deployment 151-153
creating 148-151
**management console**
accessing 28, 29
**Microsoft Application Virtualization 5.**
*See* **App-V 5**
**Microsoft Desktop Optimization**
Pack (MDOP) 3
**Microsoft Developer Network (MSDN)** 3
**Microsoft RemoteApp**
used, for publishing applications 135-138
**Microsoft Scripted Installer (MSI)**
App-V package, deploying via 102
**Microsoft Silverlight**
URL 28
**Microsoft System Centre Configuration**
Manager (SCCM)
about 2
URL 39
**Microsoft Visual C++ 2013 Redistributable**
Package
URL 24
**Microsoft Volume Licensing Service Centre**
URL 3

# N

**Network Load Balancing (NLB)** 2
**network share hosted application**
sequencing 75-78
**Notepad++**
URL 79

# O

**Ocra editor**
URL 45
**Office 2013 App-V package**
customizing 122-125
obtaining 118-120
publishing 121, 122
scripting, enabling 121, 122
**Office 2013 plugin**
sequencing 126-129

## Thank you for buying
# Microsoft Application Virtualization Cookbook

# About Packt Publishing

Packt, pronounced 'packed', published its first book, *Mastering phpMyAdmin for Effective MySQL Management*, in April 2004, and subsequently continued to specialize in publishing highly focused books on specific technologies and solutions.

Our books and publications share the experiences of your fellow IT professionals in adapting and customizing today's systems, applications, and frameworks. Our solution-based books give you the knowledge and power to customize the software and technologies you're using to get the job done. Packt books are more specific and less general than the IT books you have seen in the past. Our unique business model allows us to bring you more focused information, giving you more of what you need to know, and less of what you don't.

Packt is a modern yet unique publishing company that focuses on producing quality, cutting-edge books for communities of developers, administrators, and newbies alike. For more information, please visit our website at www.PacktPub.com.

# About Packt Enterprise

In 2010, Packt launched two new brands, Packt Enterprise and Packt Open Source, in order to continue its focus on specialization. This book is part of the Packt Enterprise brand, home to books published on enterprise software – software created by major vendors, including (but not limited to) IBM, Microsoft, and Oracle, often for use in other corporations. Its titles will offer information relevant to a range of users of this software, including administrators, developers, architects, and end users.

# Writing for Packt

We welcome all inquiries from people who are interested in authoring. Book proposals should be sent to author@packtpub.com. If your book idea is still at an early stage and you would like to discuss it first before writing a formal book proposal, then please contact us; one of our commissioning editors will get in touch with you.

We're not just looking for published authors; if you have strong technical skills but no writing experience, our experienced editors can help you develop a writing career, or simply get some additional reward for your expertise.

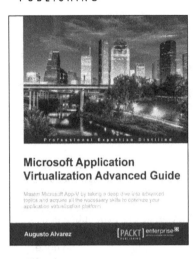

**Microsoft Application Virtualization Advanced Guide**

Master Microsoft App-V by taking a deep dive into advanced topics and acquire all the necessary skills to optimize your application virtualisation platform

Augusto Alvarez    [PACKT] enterprise

# Microsoft Application Virtualization Advanced Guide

ISBN: 978-1-84968-448-4          Paperback: 474 pages

Master Microsoft App-V by taking a deep drive into advanced topics and acquire all the necessary skills to optimize your application virtualization platform

1. Understand advanced topics in App-V; identify some rarely known components and options available in the platform.

2. Acquire advanced guidelines on how to troubleshoot App-V installations, sequencing, and application deployments.

3. Learn how to handle particular applications, adapting companys' policies to the implementation, enforcing application licenses, securing the environment, and so on.

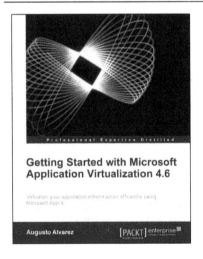

**Getting Started with Microsoft Application Virtualization 4.6**

Virtualize your application infrastructure efficiently using Microsoft App-V

Augusto Alvarez    [PACKT] enterprise

# Getting Started with Microsoft Application Virtualization 4.6

ISBN: 978-1-84968-126-1          Paperback: 308 pages

Virtualize your application infrastructure efficiently using Microsoft App-V

1. Publish, deploy, and manage your virtual applications with App-V.

2. Understand how Microsoft App-V can fit into your company.

3. Guidelines for planning and designing an App-V environment.

Please check **www.PacktPub.com** for information on our titles

Implementing
Microsoft Forefront
Unified Access
Gateway 2010
Erez Ben-Ari

[PACKT]▶

# Implementing Microsoft Forefront Unified Access Gateway 2010 [Video]

ISBN: 978-1-84968-926-7          Duration: 02:00 hours

Learn how to install and configure Microsoft UAG 2010 and take full advantage of its features

1. Covers all the product features, from installation to array management.

2. Goes through the most important and useful daily tasks an administrator needs to manage the UAG server effectively.

3. Delivered by the leading expert on Forefront UAG world-wide.

4. Provides quick and efficient training using a hands-on visual approach.

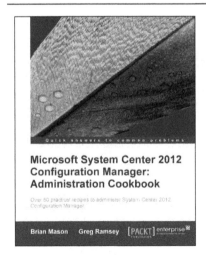

Quick answers to common problems

Microsoft System Center 2012
Configuration Manager:
Administration Cookbook

Over 50 practical recipes to administer System Center 2012
Configuration Manager

Brian Mason    Greg Ramsey    [PACKT] enterprise ⚇

# Microsoft System Center 2012 Configuration Manager: Administration Cookbook

ISBN: 978-1-84968-494-1          Paperback: 224 pages

Over 50 practical recipes to administer System Center 2012 Configuration Manager

1. Administer System Center 2012 Configuration Manager.

2. Provides fast answers to questions commonly asked by new administrators.

3. Skip the why's and go straight to the how-to's.

Please check **www.PacktPub.com** for information on our titles

www.ingramcontent.com/pod-product-compliance
Lightning Source LLC
Chambersburg PA
CBHW060555060326
40690CB00017B/3720